BABY BOOMER INVESTING

Baby Boomer Investing

Where do we go from here?

Georges Yared

C&G Group, LLC

This book is dedicated to my wife Cindy and to our starting five:
Stephanie, Ryan, Matthew, Alexandra and Joseph

Baby Boomer Investing
Copyright © 2007 Georges Yared
Published by C&G Group, LLC

For further information, please contact:
Geoyared@aol.com

Book design by:
Arbor Books, Inc.
www.arborbooks.com

Printed in the United States

Baby Boomer Investing
Georges Yared

1. Title 2. Author 3. Investments/Personal Finance

Library of Congress Control Number: 2006908093

ISBN 10: 0-9789515-1-4
ISBN 13: 978-0-9789515-1-1

TABLE OF CONTENTS

ACKNOWLEDGMENTS

AT AGE 51, I'M RIGHT IN THE MIDDLE of the Baby Boomer generation and I lean on the expertise of my fellow Boomers, both older and younger. This club of ours, with members ranging in age from 42 to 60, is something special.

I want to thank my non-Boomer fan club—my five children: Stephanie, Ryan, Matt, Alexandra and Joseph. Talk about an inspirational group of kids! Stephanie's husband Chad is like a son to me, and their beautiful daughter Bailey is, at age 10, miles ahead of where I was at age 20! She's so wise and so observant. Ryan's wife Jessica adds a daughter to our family. She is so smart and kind, and we are lucky to know her.

I am forever indebted to friends who gave me insight and wisdom while writing this book. My profound thanks go to Nancy Young; she is so honest, it sometimes hurts. I also thank Kathleen McCue; she is honest, too, but more delicate with me.

I would like to express my gratitude to Charlette Sgro—my sister, my confidante and a phenomenal broker. There are also my two other sisters—Monique, who ekes into the Baby Boomer club at age 42 and Nickie, who is not yet a member. She is too young, and I hate her for that! Both of my baby sisters were very supportive as I wrote this book.

Thank you to my dear friend Dave LaRue, who challenged me to write my first book, *Stop Losing Money Today*, and encouraged me to keep on going with this second one. Dave is a life coach and the very best in the field. His methods are inspiring.

I have to thank my friends Linda and David Johnson, who served as proofreaders and told me to keep on thinking!

I am grateful for all the wonderful people at Arbor Books in New York and New Jersey. Joel Hochman, the founder, kept me on a realistic path but told that me all things are possible. Susan Lago and James Uttel fielded all my calls and were patient and kind with me, although I know I drove them crazy sometimes—thanks to you both for putting up with me. Elise Vaz, thank you for editing my manuscript and being so patient with me as well.

As for my wife and partner Cindy: what can I say? She believed in me from the beginning and did not bat an eyelash when I told her that I wanted to become a writer. She encouraged me, and we laughed as she reminded me that I had said the same thing 20 years ago. The only question she asked was, "What took you so long?" She is the greatest mother, wife and friend anyone could ever dream of. Thanks, honey, for letting me pursue my dream.

INTRODUCTION

MY NAME IS GEORGES YARED, and I have been in the investment industry for almost 28 years. Yes, I am a Baby Boomer, and I will always capitalize those Bs because we deserve to be capitalized. We've made it! We've earned it! We have our own title for our group, so let's enjoy it and even flaunt it! How many "clubs" do you know that have 78 million members?

The oldest of the Baby Boomers are beginning their seventh decade in 2006—they'll be turning 60 this year. This includes two of our most notable members: President George W. Bush and former president Bill Clinton.

The youngest Boomers are turning 42 this year. This incredible generation brought us the hippies of the late 1960s, the joggers of the 70s and 80s, the computer geeks of the 90s and some brand new grandparents in the early 2000s.

This Baby Boomer generation has seen the greatest creation of wealth in the history of the United States. We have experienced a stock market bull run that began in August 1982 and still continues as of this writing. Remember, the Dow Jones sat at 780 in August 1982, but it has been hovering around the 12,000 mark here in 2006. The stock market has basically 15-folded in 24 years.

We have seen the evolvement of some small "growth" companies who have become mainstay businesses in our daily lives. From Microsoft, Cisco, Google and Yahoo to Costco, Chipotle and Nike, these companies have even created new words for our vocabulary.

Our homes have skyrocketed in value these past 20 years. Depending on your location, values have increased anywhere from 4 to 15 times. If you have been able to afford a second house, chances are you chose one on an ocean or lake, in a warm climate or maybe in the mountains; statistically, those are the things us Baby Boomers like in our homes-away-from-home.

Congress enacted the 401(k) plan and various forms of the individual retirement account (IRA) in the past 25 years, allowing us to save for retirement on a tax-advantaged basis. We can also save, tax advantaged, for our children's and grandchildren's college educations with the 529 college savings plans. As big corporations avoid and even liquidate their pension plans, we'll see 401(k)s and IRAs become more important in our overall planning.

One issue I will address in greater detail later in this book is our critical need to revamp the Social Security system. But guess what? That doesn't apply to us. Social Security will be there and be solvent for our needs; it's our children and grandchildren that might have to go without. In light of that, it's time to put the politics aside and seriously discuss the alternatives and possible outcomes. Remember: not for us, but for our heirs.

Many of us Boomers have lost or are losing our parents. Mine passed away in 2000 and 2001, leaving me a 46-year-old orphan. The good news is that many of our parents are living longer and better, having qualities of life that I don't think they even imagined. My in-laws, both in their 70s, are computer smart—always emailing and IMing my wife and me. They exercise and eat healthful meals.

Where Do We Go From Here?

This book is about investing for our futures and for our children's and grandchildren's futures. But I think that before we look forward, we have to understand how we got here.

As I mentioned, this generation has witnessed and been part of the greatest wealth creation. Many of the great companies formed in the 70s, 80s and 90s have seen their stock market values explode and provide great wealth. Also, many of the older American companies reinvented themselves and provided their shareholders with wealth creation.

Some, of course, didn't "get it" and ended up on the ash heap. In the 2000s, we have seen some terrible corporate scandals and excesses, but fortunately many sensible regulations and systems have been put in place to prevent future abuses, or at least curtail them. CEOs and CFOs must clearly account for their numbers before they are released to the public. Boards of directors are also on the hot seat, and their liability can be personal.

But where do we go from here? This book will discuss the major trends in healthcare, lifestyle, technology and communications, and alternative energy. We will explore how we got to where we are and, more importantly, where we are going.

We'll also look at what great companies will help us create future wealth and comfortable lifestyles for our families.

Enjoy this book—I believe you will learn some great investing ideas and enjoy some of its trips down memory lane.

Please feel free to email me any of your funny stories, experiences or ideas at memories@investingbabyboomer.com.

Also, please come and join me at my Website—www.investingbabyboomer.com. It's just for us Boomers, with specific stock and stock fund ideas, as well as commentary about the markets and what affects us. I'll also include interviews with some of the world's best portfolio managers and strategists.

This book has various company recommendations that are

appropriate at the time of this writing July 2006. Please consult your advisors before investing in any of the recommended names. So, Boomers, sit back and relax…and enjoy this book.

CHAPTER ONE

NOW AND THEN...THEN AND NOW

IN EARLY JUNE 1973, I was a newly minted high school graduate. I had turned 18 in April, had a steady girlfriend, was going off to college and had the rest of my life in front of me. Man, life was good. My bell-bottoms were hip and my collar-length hair was thick and curly. Doesn't get much better than that!

A week after graduation, my mother told me in her heavy French accent, "Uncle Ed *ees* coming over for a *Frrwench-kooked deenner* and has a *geeft* for you."

I thought to myself, *I hope his gift has at least one zero—hopefully two—after the first number.* After all, an 18-year-old can never have enough cash in his pockets!

The Best Gift Ever

When Uncle Ed came to the house he had a wrapped box with him, not an envelope. *Damn*, I thought. *It's a real gift, not cash or a check.* Oh well. It was the thought that counted, right?

After we exchanged all the pleasantries and opened the first bottle of wine, we sat down to a scrumptious, *Frrwench-kooked deenner*. When we were done eating, Uncle Ed reached under the table, pulled out the wrapped box and handed it over to me.

I graciously accepted it—hey, I had good manners!—and the excitement on his face was like a kid on Christmas morning. I began to think, *Who is this gift for? Him or me?*

Both of my parents and my older sister surrounded me. You would have thought Uncle Ed had handed me the keys to a new car. Well, I opened the box and to my surprise, it was one of those new inventions: a handheld calculator.

Wow! I thought, taking it carefully out of the box. The calculator was made by Texas Instruments, and it was about seven inches long and four inches wide. The keys on the pad were about the size of a nickel, and it did the four basic math functions: addition, subtraction, multiplication and division.

I had recently mastered a slide rule in my senior year, and I'd thought that made me pretty smart. But now I thought, *Where do I fit?* The nerds had their slide rules in their plastic pocket protectors, but I had a calculator. A real calculator! *Cool group, here I come!* I thought—though I vowed to still talk to my nerd friends.

This Texas Instruments calculator cost $69. I knew that because Uncle Ed had left the price tag on the box. He had a habit of doing that! It was a lot of money in 1973, especially for a high school graduation gift. In 2006, that $69 would be worth maybe $400.

I was very excited about and appreciative of this gift. Calculators were just hitting the market and they were certainly considered a luxury. Plus, I thought, what a cool company name: *Texas Instruments*. I thought maybe the company made drums, guitars, saxophones and trumpets, and then made calculators on the side!

Naïve as I was, I thought "chips" were something you put

dip on, not little pieces of silicone that carried out specific functions and made this calculator work effortlessly.

Nonetheless, I showed that calculator off to all my friends. We were all so amazed by how fast the answers appeared after hitting the "equal" sign. The first test I ran on the calculator—I'll never forget—was 1973 times 1973. I hit the equal sign and 3,892,729 appeared in less than a second!

Amazing! I thought. *This little baby should make college math and science classes so much easier.* I thought that maybe I could rent it out to my friends in college and make a little money. I wondered if professors would even let me use it in class—or more importantly, on exams. Oh well...I figured I'd find out come September.

Who We Are, Where We've Been

Baby Boomers. There are approximately 78 million of us in the United States. We were born between 1946 and 1964; I was born right in the middle, in 1955.

We are more educated than any generation before us. We are consumers of enormous amounts of information and goods and services—more than any generation before us. We are the children of the "greatest generation" and the grandchildren of millions of immigrants who ended up in the United States. Our children are growing up with more advantages than any other generation, and the same can be said about our grandchildren.

Since my high school graduation 33 years ago, we have witnessed massive advances in our country and the world. The ensuing chapters will cover the major stories and give you some advice about where to invest for further and future growth.

Almost every industry has gone through transformations and improvements in efficiencies. Also, due to major technological advances, we have seen the creation of new industries that have gone on to really thrive. The Internet alone has spawned some large companies, such as Yahoo, Google and Monster.com.

During these past 33 years, we have witnessed the decline of American-based manufacturing and the pain associated with those job losses and displacements. We will not be able to compete with China, India and Third World nations on the labor front.

But on the flip side, as we have migrated to a services-based economy, millions upon millions of new, different jobs have been created. As a generation, we are comfortable with the global economy. We transact in this international market-place every day—driving our Toyotas, watching football games on our Sony HDTVs and taking digital pictures with our Nikon cameras.

I have been very fortunate, as my work has kept me right in the middle of all these advances and changes. I spent 1979 through 1991 with Dean Witter Reynolds (now Morgan Stanley—more change) working with individual investors. During that time, I also managed two different branch offices for Dean Witter, one major region and even a country (Canada).

I was part of the beginning of the bull market in 1982, which is still going on as you read this book. I saw many new companies become public; I saw many succeed, many fail and many get acquired.

I witnessed a couple of nerds from the Seattle, Washington, area drop out of Harvard University—nobody drops out of Harvard!—and form a bizarre company called Microsoft. They actually took on IBM for control of the personal computer operating system market. Imagine what these guys—we now know them as Bill Gates and Paul Allen—would have accomplished had they finished college!

I was able to witness a company go public that would actually let our computers talk to each other, let us share files and information and eventually let us hook up to some new-fangled thing called the Internet. That company was Cisco Systems.

I had the privilege of watching a medical device company revolutionize cardiac care by testing and receiving U.S. Food and Drug Administration (FDA) approval for implantable cardiac pacemakers and defibrillators. That company was Medtronic.

The list goes on and on.

From 1992 through 2002, I was a partner at a research-boutique investment banking firm called Wessels, Arnold and Henderson (acquired by Dain Rauscher in 1998; Dain was then acquired by The Royal Bank of Canada, changing our name to RBC Dain in 2000). At Wessels, I was involved with our European accounts in London, Paris, Geneva and Zurich. These accounts traded in American stocks and valued our growth research. I also had the privilege of getting to know and advise a few hundred U.S. growth companies.

In January 2003, I joined ThinkEquity Partners as a partner. The company was headquartered in San Francisco, and I was in charge of the European markets. Again, I was also involved in advising several growth companies.

Jumping Into the Global Marketplace

Let's take a brief trip down Memory Lane. We are old enough to remember…My first year of college started in September 1973. I'll never forget our student lounge, which featured a new, revolutionary game called "air hockey." Man, we spent hours playing. We held student tournaments and we discovered that it was a great way to meet girls.

That was our entertainment in 1973. We had no video games (Pac-Man wasn't introduced until 1980), no cell phones, not even a portable cassette player. What's a CD? Never heard of it. An iPod? Was that a science experiment? We had air hockey; that was our entertainment.

Over spring break in 1974, three of my buddies and I drove to Fort Lauderdale, Florida, from Cleveland, Ohio, for some sunshine and relaxation. My parents had given me a brand new car as a high school graduation gift, so of course that was how we got there.

The car was...are you ready for this?...a Peugeot 504. My mother was French, so she wanted me to have a French car. It was a four-door beauty, with leather interior (at least, I think it was leather) and a bright green exterior; it was just a really cool car.

There were very few imports in the United States back then. People tended to "buy American"—or so I learned as we were driving from Fort Lauderdale back to Ohio.

I was behind the wheel and my buddies were sound asleep, and sure enough, a state trooper pulled me over. I think I was speeding. The United States had just adopted the 55 miles per hour speed limit to answer our "first oil crisis."

The state trooper, I'll never forget, had a nametag that read "Wilbur." I figured I would use my charm to get out of this possible infraction.

"Good morning, Officer—is it *Wilbur*? How are you this morning?" I said cheerfully, smiling as I looked up at him.

"License and registration, boy," he barked at me. "And what the hell kinda car is this?"

"Well, sir...it is Officer Wilbur, correct? It's a Peugeot 504, French made."

"It's a what?"

"A Peugeot, sir." I began to worry, as his face was turning

10

different shades of red. "Aaa...*Pugget*?!" he said loudly, screwing his face up in consternation.

"Yes, sir, it's a Pugget; that would be the other name for it!" I said, still trying win him over with my charm and congeniality.

"Boy, down here in St. Lucie County, Florida, we buy American. Now get the hell outta here and slow down!"

"Yes sir, and thank you for your kind consideration and—"

"Get outta here!" he yelled, and I did just that.

I don't think Officer Wilbur had yet grasped that we were truly entering the global marketplace. The influx of foreign cars into the United States really began in the 1970s. New names entered into our vocabulary: Datsun (now Nissan), Toyota, Mercedes-Benz, BMW and so on.

Our parents' generation was more into buying American and keeping Americans employed. I had a college professor who told me that I personally cost one American job by having this "foreign Frenchy car." I felt pretty guilty until I remembered that he taught zoology and not business.

As a nation, we tended to export more than we imported back then. That trend began to shift quite dramatically as we became a net importer.

There was a high degree of pride in our parents' generation that our products were the envy of the world. The expression "global economy" had not yet been coined, though—neither had "Baby Boomers"—and so our products were primarily American made.

Remember the Admiral and RCA TV sets? Magnavox was a big manufacturer of hi-fis (gosh, when was the last time you heard the word *hi-fi*?) and TVs as well. Our record albums were 33? rpm, which replaced the old 45s and the really old 78s.

My kids think I'm speaking Greek when I mention numbers like those. They've grown up with CDs and now, of course, MP3 downloads. My 14-year-old found an old box of my record albums in our storage room and seriously asked me, "Dad, what are these?"

He was even more quizzical when I tried to explain how those "things" were played on a "turntable."

"So, how could you bike or go to the beach with all this heavy stuff?" he asked, and I pictured my old record player strapped to my upper arm, like he wears his iPod today. Man, I felt old!

A while ago, my 16-year-old daughter was doing a history report using our family computer. I asked if I could help, proudly reminding her that I was a history buff and got "A"s in all my high school and college history courses.

She said, "No thanks, Dad. I'm just Googling for the information that I need."

I went on to tell her that "we" went to the library back in our day and that Googling was something toddlers did! All of a sudden I felt like my grandmother telling me about her daily seven-mile walk to school—it was uphill both ways, too! Times, they are a-changin'!

The Communication Revolution

The U.S population in 1970 was approximately 200 million to 205 million, and in 2006 we are approaching 300 million. According to the Centers for Disease Control (CDC), we will approach 400 million by the year 2050. Our nation will virtually double its population in just 80 years.

Our life expectancy is now 77.5 years for males and 80.4 for females (also according to the CDC). That life expectancy should gently nudge up as we Baby Boomers hit our 60s and 70s, as we are the generation with the finest healthcare available.

Our children and grandchildren, we hope, will live even longer than our generation, although many healthcare professionals are worried about our young people not getting enough exercise and proper nutrition. In fact, many worry that our kids may have a shorter life expectancy than we do.

"Too many video games and not enough bicycles," as my doctor simply explained to me.

Sadly, many of us have lost our parents, but others of us have vibrant, active parents in their 70s and 80s. The "greatest generation" has embraced exercise, good nutrition and preventative healthcare (which we'll discuss in a later chapter). Many are playing tennis or golf, or bicycling daily.

My 75-year-old mother-in-law is an active participant at the Curves health club. She is in fabulous shape, both physically and mentally. Everywhere she travels she picks up the local phone book and finds out where the nearest Curves is located. She takes her water bottle and goes for a workout with pleasure. Talk about discipline!

Communication in this world of ours has become instant. You may remember how back in our college days, Sunday night was "call home night"—though it could have more accurately been called "*collect* call home night."

The call was normally made from the pay phone (remember pay phones?) down the hall in the dorm. We'd catch up with our parents and siblings, and of course, ask Mom and Dad for more money!

Today, my 14-year-old has a cell phone, and he was the second-to-last person in his class to get one. What a negligent parent I have been!

If we really want to understand where we've come from, here's a story that crystallizes it: in September 2005, I was visiting my clients in London. I was in a meeting with Mr. Skeptic, a professional money manager who loathed technology and yearned for the good old days—whatever those were.

It was 3:30 p.m. London time, which was 9:30 a.m. Central Time in the United States. My cell phone rang, and by looking at the caller ID (another thing Mr. Skeptic hated), I could see it was my daughter. I normally don't take calls when in a meeting, but seeing who it was, I thought I'd better answer it.

Quickly telling Mr. Skeptic that it was my daughter, I flipped open my phone and asked Alexandra what was up. She was calling from school—on her cell phone, of course—quickly explaining to me that she couldn't reach Mom, so she decided to call me.

She wanted to know if she could spend $25 on a volleyball sweatshirt at the bookstore. They only had one left! After quickly saying yes (what a sap), I told her I couldn't talk because I was in a meeting.

We hung up, and Mr. Skeptic was actually impressed. "You mean that was your daughter calling you from Minneapolis, her cell phone to yours, asking something so simple? And she made that call like it was normal and no big deal?"

He was blown away to the point where he thought that maybe he should look at some communication stocks. Man, what a rocket scientist!

But just think of the evolution in communication these past 33 years: from me calling my mom and dad collect 30 years ago to my daughter calling me on my cell phone, from her cell phone, 4,500 miles and an ocean away. And, her call to me was cheaper than my collect call home to my parents, who were 400 miles away! It's amazing when you really think about it.

Text Messages, the Internet and Beyond

Another example: in spring 2006, my son and I were in Florida, where he was attending a baseball camp. It so happened that another British client of mine, Mr. Wow, was in Orlando with his family on vacation (or as the British say, "on holiday"). I called him "Mr. Wow" because that was his usual reaction to most investment stories.

We were all out to dinner one night, and my son's cell phone was emitting some funky ring tone every 10 minutes, signaling new text messages coming in. Finally, I asked him to take it outside because it was becoming annoying to my client and his wife. I gently reminded Joey that these clients were paying for his braces and his future smile.

As Joey was leaving the table, Mr. Wow asked him who kept calling. Turning a bit red in the face, Joey said it was a "friend" from school. I knew right away that the "friend" was a lovely 14-year-old girl who my son was keen on.

Mr. Wow then asked if she was in Florida as well. Joey explained that she was actually on vacation with her family in Hawaii. Mr. Wow was absolutely...wowed! This "friend" was a good 5,000 miles and five time zones away from where we were, texting my son with her lunch review as we were finishing dinner!

What really blew Mr. Wow away was that I was not paying extra on the phone bill, since unlimited texting was included in the Verizon family plan. These two kids were carrying on a text conversation at will, with no additional cost. Mrs. Wow found the whole thing quite romantic.

What is even more remarkable is our ability to e-mail back and forth around the world in seconds. My father came from a small village in Lebanon that had 12 phones *total*. When he moved to Ohio, he would call his brother in Lebanon and hope not to have a scratchy, constantly interrupted line. So often, the line would just go dead after a minute or two—and this was in 1998!

Later, my uncle informed my father that he had a new computer with an AOL address. Amazingly, these two brothers who could never finish a good conversation, let alone a good joke, were then e-mailing each other, carrying on uninterrupted conversations—and finally able to get to the punch lines.

The Internet has given us the ability to be social with total strangers. There are chat rooms on nearly any subject. My sister-in-law was pregnant recently, and she joined a chat room with a lot of other expectant mothers. These women would talk about their nutritional needs, the physical limitations of their pregnancies and just about any other subject having to do with expecting a baby.

These women were from all over the United States and many were using "screen names" versus their real names, so they remained anonymous. I really wanted to meet "Bowling Ball Mamma"!

With the Internet, we can uncover just about any information in the world, on just about any subject. We'll cover more on this subject later, in the "lifestyle" chapter.

The strides made in the last 33 years will probably pale in comparison to where we are going. Our healthcare, lifestyle, technology and communications, and alternative energy will only get better and still more efficient.

I hope that this book will highlight where we are going and how to profit from these innovations and technologies. Many "old economy" companies have reinvented themselves or changed their business models to compete effectively in 2006 and beyond. Also, many newer companies will be discussed, as some have great opportunities to become huge, game-changing players in the ensuing years.

I am very fortunate that I have many friends who are among the best professional money managers and analysts in the world. These people quite often have chances to see today what is coming tomorrow. I will share with you in this book many of the insights these professionals have observed, as well as what they are invested in or about to invest in.

For continuous updates on the companies discussed in this book—as well as many additional companies that we haven't discussed—I invite you to visit my website, www.investing-babyboomer.com, where you'll find their current prospects, earnings outlooks, valuation analyses, competitive advantages and disadvantages, expected news, and more.

CHAPTER TWO

THE CARDINAL RULES

IN MY EARLIER BOOK, *Stop Losing Money Today*, I highlighted many important cardinal rules of investing. First and foremost: it's your money, your nest egg, that is necessary to secure your future and the future of your loved ones.

Two things we cannot outsource are health and money. We can seek outside advice on these two important aspects of our lives, but we are ultimately responsible and must monitor our own progress or lack of progress in both areas.

Too many times in my career, I've seen investors outsource their money affairs only to be burned or aggravated, and the same can happen when you hand over your personal affairs to others. No one cares more for your future—and your future comfort—than you and your family. Accountability starts with you and then spreads out to those who are advising or helping you.

I cannot tell you how many times I had to arbitrate a dispute between a client and his or her broker/adviser because there was a lack of communication. Most complaints fell into the "I didn't understand what I bought" or "It was never fully explained to me" categories.

When a stock is recommended to you and you accept the

idea to buy or sell it, you take on the ownership of the idea as much as your broker does. Frankly, you take on more because it is *your* money.

Interviewing Your Broker

You should select your broker/adviser as carefully as you select your doctor. Do not be impressed by titles along—*e.g.*, senior vice president, first vice president or senior adviser. These are granted through commission production, and commission production only. They are not given out for superior performance or for protecting clients' assets from bad ideas or lack of communication.

I have met several "senior vice presidents" who were horrible stock pickers or who didn't do very well for their clients. They built their businesses by bringing in two or three new clients a week, while another one or two were lost out the back door.

I have also met many senior and first vice presidents who have been fantastic. They listened to their clients, cared deeply about their futures and truly built long-lasting, profitable relationships with them.

Whether you're re-evaluating your existing broker or a looking at potential new one, it is key that you interview him or her. Remember, it's *your* money you want them to handle.

Interviewing your broker is a simple process. You want to know his or her investment philosophy. Sounds simple, but it can be very revealing. Consider questions such as: is your broker growth oriented? Averse to risk? Fixed-income oriented? Is your broker all about packaged products (mutual funds, annuities, insurance products), or does he or she favor individual stocks, or both? To what degree?

What is the broker's philosophy on asset allocation (percentages in cash, stocks, mutual funds, insurance products and so on)? How often does he or she initiate communication or conduct a portfolio review?

Another area of questioning that is important for your existing or potential broker is about his or her firm's research department (assuming the firm has one; if not, find out what your broker's research sources are). Ask your broker who his or her favorite analysts are and what their track record of performance has been.

All too often, here is what happens: the broker calls you and says, "Our analyst likes ABC Corp. at $12 and thinks it will go to $18 to $20."

And here is the classic response from clients: "Well, if your analyst likes it and you think it's okay, then go ahead and buy it."

Wrong! Never! The idea may be terrific and work out exactly as predicted, but there must be a bit of homework done first.

Here is a list of questions to ask before agreeing to the idea or not. This takes a whole five minutes! Start with:

"Tell me about this analyst."

"What is the analyst's track record for the last five recommendations?"

"How long has your analyst been an analyst?"

You need to know if this analyst has a record of success and timeliness. Ask if there is a report—preferably an initiation report—on the company that this person is recommending. Initiation reports tend to be more thorough and detail the company and its positioning within its universe. Quarterly updates are shorter and assume a certain degree of knowledge about the company.

Whichever is available, ask your broker to e-mail it to you.

You may not read it, but by asking, you can be sure your broker will read it thoroughly.

Another important question to ask your broker: is the analyst from the industry he or she writes about, or from the Master of Business Administration (MBA) track? Or both? I'll take an analyst from industry almost every time. Why? Because that person tends to better understand the dynamics, *and* his or her Rolodex is full of contacts.

Finally, I would ask the broker if the analyst has a "theme piece" about the industry, and where this specific recommendation fits in. A good, thoughtful analyst will have an industry theme report highlighting the dynamics of the industry, who the key players are, who is moving up or down and what expectations are for the next one to three years.

The idea here is not to play a game of "gotcha" but to build the accountability line. If you are serious about your investments, you want your broker to be as serious about and dedicated to your objectives as you are.

Analyzing Your Interests

With this dedication comes the fleshing out of specific recommendations and where they should fit into your portfolio. If the stock idea works out as planned, the broker, the analyst and you can all take a victory lap. If the idea doesn't work out for whatever reason, the last thing you should hear is your broker blaming the analyst.

Too many times I've heard, "I never liked that analyst anyway." That statement means minimal or no homework was done. Inexcusable!

Similar analyses should be completed for mutual fund investments as well. Not all growth funds, aggressive growth funds and growth and income funds are created equal. They are managed by a professional portfolio manager and a team of assistants.

You need to inquire about the track record and qualifications of the portfolio manager. How many years has the manager run the fund? Hopefully the answer will be "at least 5 years." Why? Because the last 5 to 10 years have been tumultuous and volatile in the U.S. stock markets.

Did this manager outperform from 1996 to 2001? Or did this manager outperform in the tough years of 2001 and 2002? At a minimum, you want a three-year record. Any portfolio manager can have a great year or a slump year, but three years' performance compared with the market should be enough time to firmly establish a trend.

Ask your broker to draw out a timeline on the mutual fund's performance versus the S&P 500 for the last 5 to 10 years if the fund is a general growth fund. If it's an aggressive growth fund, or if it's specifically invested in small to mid-cap names, ask for that same timeline versus the NASDAQ Composite and/or the Russell 2000.

These two indices are great trackers of the emerging growth stocks and are typically populated by the smaller capitalized stocks. The data is easily available and compiling it will not be difficult or time-consuming. But remember, it's *your* money, and the accountability line must be established!

Set Your Price Targets

Another cardinal rule: one of the important things to do before buying a stock is to establish a price target. The price target should be for both upside and downside. Does this mean that you should sell the stock automatically? No, it doesn't.

What it should do is trigger a conversation about the stock or fund. Are the fundamentals still intact? Is the growth rate still the same, or going higher or contracting? Was the recent quarterly earnings report in line with expectations, or better or worse?

Professional portfolio managers normally use price targets on all their stocks. Example: Dr. Michael Mullaney, now retired but formerly of Threadneedle Investments in London, ran a multibillion-dollar portfolio of mostly growth stocks. He had a price target for every stock, both upside and downside. It caused me to have many, many conversations with him over the years—some not so pleasant.

Dr. Mullaney moved his price target on Cisco Systems 34 times before he sold one share! Moving the target as often as he did caused us to re-evaluate the fundamentals each time.

Dr. Mullaney was more emphatic about downside protection. If he bought a stock at $20 and it went down to $17, he would review all the fundamentals as if it were a brand new idea. At that point he would determine whether to do nothing, to sell it because things had changed, or to buy more because the fundamentals had been reinforced.

The same technique applies to stock mutual funds. Rather than a specific price target, the metric should be percentage up or down versus the comparable universe. If the NASDAQ Composite is up 12 percent so far this year, but your fund is up only 8 percent, questions need to be asked.

With a mutual fund, normally the portfolio is updated quarterly on the fund's Website; some, however, do it monthly. You or your broker should examine the portfolio to see if any specific stocks are dragging down the performance.

Conversely, if your fund is outperforming its comparable universe, check out the portfolio to see what stocks are leading the way.

The final message here, whether you own stocks or mutual funds, is to communicate with your broker/adviser as often as necessary. It's *your* money, so be an advocate for it!

Love Your Family, Not Your Stocks

Another important cardinal rule is checking your emotions at the door. These are stocks or mutual funds, not your children or grandchildren. There is no falling in love with a company! No, *non, nyet, verboten!*

As I detailed in *Stop Losing Money Today*, falling in love with a company is bad—in my case it was VeriSign Corp., which cost me $2 million. Maybe if I'd had a dollar for every time I heard, "Yeah, it's a *great* company," I could have recouped some of that lost fortune.

Respectfully admire where a company is in its development cycle, but don't fall in love with it. Many of us love TiVo as a consumer product, but do we want to own the stock? Not really. I love my iPod, and as soon as I learn how to use it, I'll *really* love it, but do I want to own its maker, Apple Computer? Actually, yes, but we'll get to that a few chapters later.

Your investment decisions must be made with a keen sense of where the company is going—not where it has been.

We all admire the accomplishments of Wal-Mart, Microsoft, General Electric, Pfizer Pharmaceuticals and Cisco Systems. These are the titans of the last 20 to 30 years. Their individual stock prices and market capitalization (all the outstanding shares of a company multiplied by a share's current price) reflect what they have achieved in consistent earnings, cash build-up, franchise value and market share over the years.

If you owned any one of these stocks over the years, chances are you have done very, very well, but that previous success was in their price and valuation! Where do you go from here?

Keeping emotional detachment in mind, do I think Wal-Mart (WMT), currently with a $200 billion market cap, can double or triple its value? I'm not sure; that would be quite a challenge.

But I am pretty sure that Costco (COST), with a current market cap of $24 billion and executing superbly, can grow to a $100 billion market cap. You must do this analysis with all your stocks or stock funds.

Another example: Microsoft (MSFT) has been one of the greatest wealth creators of the past 20 years. The stock was a rocket ship in the late 1980s and throughout the 90s. At one point, the company hit a market cap of $500 billion, but it now sits at $240 billion. Still, it's got stunning returns for investors who bought the shares in the early 90s.

I tip my hat to the incredible vision the Microsoft management team executed over the past 20 years. I stand in awe of the jobs they created—all 64,000-plus of them. I am flabbergasted by the billions and billions in federal and local taxes the company has paid. Just like millions of others, I am grateful for its products, which make using my personal computer simpler and more user-friendly.

But would I buy Microsoft stock today? Personally, no, I would not. The company's ability to grow its revenues and earnings from here on are much more challenging than for some other software companies. As Microsoft looks to expand into the entertainment and search engine fields, its dominance is questionable. After all, it will have to compete with Google (GOOG) and Sony (SNE), two very tough and very entrenched competitors.

I believe I can earn better and bigger returns elsewhere in the software universe. The stock market recognizes and rewards growth. Past performance does not guarantee future success!

It's the Cap, Not the Price, That Matters

Another cardinal rule is: do not get hung up on a particular stock's price. Get hung up on the company's market capitalization instead.

Again, market capitalization (cap) is all the outstanding shares of a company multiplied by a share's current price. For example, TiVo has a market cap of $535 million; that is, 85,816,000 total shares outstanding times the current price of $6.23, which equals a $535 million market cap.

Another example: Google has a market cap of $112 billion, which is 297,770,000 total shares outstanding times the current price of $376. The market cap tells you what the enterprise is currently valued at in the stock market.

As you examine a company for either buying or selling, ask your broker/adviser where the market cap can go from here. Analysts usually make it simple by publishing a price target on the stock; for example, stock at $20 with a buy rating and a price target of $28 within 12 months.

That's fine and dandy, but what is the enterprise worth and what can it be worth in the months and years to come? Remember, the stock market will move the value of a company up when it demonstrates growth on its revenues and earnings.

It is important to couple those two—revenues and earnings. A company can temporarily drive its earnings up by cost cutting, but as an investor, you want to see revenue increases causing the earnings to rise. Financial engineering will take a company only so far.

Another critical factor I like to see is a company formally

buying back its own shares in the open market. What does that mean? If a company is cash rich, as a shareholder you want that cash deployed toward either continuing to build the business or buying back and retiring some outstanding shares. The latter is normally a way for a company to signal confidence to the investing world—it's like saying that it believes in its own prospects and value.

Also, with a reduced number of shares in the marketplace, the earnings dollars are spread over fewer shares, and therefore the earnings per share take a nice jump up.

Example: Company ABC has 10 million total shares outstanding. It also has $50 million in cash on its balance sheet. Analysts expect ABC to earn $1 per share in earnings for 2006. At the beginning of 2006, Company ABC announces a share buyback program for 5 percent of its total shares, or 500,000 shares to be bought and retired.

Now, the outstanding share count becomes 9,500,000, but the earnings are now spread over fewer shares, resulting in $1.05 in earnings per share versus the expected $1.00. If this gets a bit confusing, don't get hung up on the math—just understand the concept that company share buybacks are a good thing!

Don't Ignore the Growth

The asset allocation cardinal rule: As Baby Boomer investors, we have to think about our own personal asset allocations. Where do we put our investable dollars? At age 51, I have my non–real estate dollars 65 percent in growth stocks and 35 percent in growth and income funds. No individual stock makes up more than 7 percent of my portfolio.

Why? I don't want all my eggs in one basket. I believe I own all winners in my portfolio—companies that are executing and growing their revenues, earnings and market shares—but funny things can happen. Situations can change quickly, and the stock market has a way of resetting values in an instant.

Conventional wisdom (whatever that is) says we should have exposure to cash and fixed-income bond funds. I respectfully disagree with that concept, especially if you are still working and earning income.

If you are talking about the monies that are earmarked for living expenses, mortgage payments or the tuition bills due next month, those funds should be kept in an interest bearing checking or savings account. Immediate obligations should not be in the stock market or in mutual funds.

That being said, your investible dollars, retirement plans and long-term college funds should be in growth mutual funds or individual stocks—or both.

Why? Bond market investments—whether corporate, government or municipal bonds—are normally priced at $1,000, pay a specified interest rate (typically twice a year) and mature, or pay off, at $1,000. There is no capital growth, just twice-a-year income.

It is true that during a bond's lifetime, it can fluctuate in underlying value as much as 10 to 20 percent, but it ultimately matures at $1,000. If current income from your investments is necessary, then I strongly suggest you have a portfolio with high-paying dividend stocks such as Citigroup (C), which pays a current dividend with a yield of 3.9 percent or Bank of America (BAC), which pays a current dividend of 4 percent.

While you may earn a higher interest rate on a taxable corporate or government bond, three things are working against you: one, the interest is taxed at your full tax bracket rate; two, the interest will not go up during the life of the bond; and three, there will be no growth of your capital.

With a high-paying dividend stock, three good things can happen: one, the dividend is taxed at the 15 percent rate regardless of your individual tax bracket; two, good companies have a history of raising their dividend payments (Citigroup has done so for the last five years); and three, the value of the stock over the years will more than likely rise.

Also, dividends are normally paid four times a year, whereas bond interest payments are twice a year. As we Boomers get closer to retirement, owning stocks that pay healthy dividends will provide the incomes we need, and there are many excellent growth and income mutual funds that do the same.

To really drive home the idea that as we approach retirement we cannot ignore growth, here is a real example that I was very involved with. In 1992, my parents retired from their medical jobs—Dad was a doctor and Mom was a nurse. They had accumulated about $800,000 in their pension and profit-sharing plans, all of which was rolled over into an IRA rollover account.

Their accountant (Johnny No Sense) advised them to put the whole amount into individual bonds and bond funds. When my parents asked me what I thought, I told them to get a new accountant!

They had a fabulous broker (not me, but actually my sister Charlette) who constructed their portfolio so that they could draw monthly income—about $5,000 at first—and not touch the principal. In fact, Charlette managed their portfolio so that by 2000, the value was $1,300,000 and they had increased their monthly withdrawals to $7,000.

With high-quality growth and growth with income stocks and mutual funds, my parents were able to give themselves a raise in monthly income, and their underlying value grew 50 percent in seven years! Had they listened to Johnny No Sense, the $800,000 would have been worth $800,000 in seven years and their income would have been stagnant at about $5,000 per month. The only way to have increased their monthly income would have been to sell some bonds, thus beginning the decline of their principal.

The lesson here—the cardinal rule—is that as we begin to approach our actual retirements, growth cannot be put on the back burner. Most brokers are taught like the emergency room physician: first do no harm. The harm is ignoring growth and the power that growth provides.

In my parents' case, the growth of their underlying value afforded them the opportunity to give themselves a monthly raise and not touch their principal!

As I stated in *Stop Losing Money Today*, I cannot guarantee you that the stock market will be up in the next 12 months. I can intelligently guess as I examine earnings trends in U.S. corporations, the movement of interest rates, the price movement of oil and so on if the stock market will look good, tepid or even down. But these are truly just educated guesses.

Over the past 27-plus years, I have had many "gut feelings" that frankly have been more right than any technical or fundamental data. One thing I will guarantee is that over the next 5, 10, 15 and 20 years, the value of well-thought out and well-planned portfolios will be substantially up in value. This is why long-term monies should be invested in growth funds and growth stocks.

We will have, as we have already seen in our own country and elsewhere, many major changes, scary events and crises. In the past 30 years, we witnessed the fall of the Berlin Wall, the assassination attempt on President Reagan, the Asian currency crisis, Gulf Wars I and II, showdowns with the Chinese and the Soviets, the highest interest rates recorded in modern

America (in the early 1980s), devastating hurricanes, 9/11 and many more earth-shattering events.

Yet, the value of the U.S. equities markets has marshaled through and values are far higher today than in 1980 or 1990. The year 2000 valuations were absurdly high as we went through the bubble period, but at this writing in summer 2006, those values have been recouped with much more solidification beneath them!

The cardinal rule is to buy great growth companies and/or great growth mutual funds and monitor them closely—and then watch them grow in value.

Keep reviewing the important questions. Why am I holding this stock? Are the fundamentals improving or deteriorating? Is the growth rate of revenues and earnings holding as planned or accelerating?

Further, is the portfolio manager of your fund doing the right things to keep pace with or even outpace the market? Is your broker/adviser keeping you informed and reviewing your portfolio as necessary? Is any American or world event affecting the value of your investments? If so, is it short term or long term?

Keep asking, keep your emotions in check and as we Baby Boomers age—gracefully, of course—grow your nest egg with thoughtful, well-planned out growth stocks and mutual funds.

Let's have some fun now. The ensuing chapters will detail major trends in both the United States' economy and those of the rest of the world. These chapters will focus on the topics and companies that affect us, the Baby Boomers. What are the great companies that we should be aware of, invest in, and have fun watching develop?

Some will surprise you, as they are already household names, large and established but continuing to reinvent themselves and compete effectively in their marketplaces.

Many others will be new and exciting companies that have opportunities to redefine an industry or create a new industry—or they just happen to be cool and interesting. We will look at healthcare firms, lifestyle businesses, technology and communication outfits and alternative energy companies.

For continuous updates on these companies and advice on knowing when to buy or sell, plus news and events, price target information and more, please refer to my website, www.investingbabyboomer.com, where I will also review and update the cardinal rules of investing in further detail.

CHAPTER THREE

HEALTHCARE: THE COMPANIES THAT WILL CHANGE OUR LIVES

IN EARLY 2006, I had the privilege of going through the Mayo Clinic's executive physical program. Fortunately, I have had very few medical problems in my life; other than an arthroscopic knee surgery in 1988 and a double hernia operation when I was five years old, I have never spent a night in a hospital.

I have been blessed with good genetics, and I do take care of myself. But I could not pass up the opportunity for a head-to-toe examination at the world-renowned Mayo Clinic.

Visiting the World's Most Famous Clinic

Rochester, Minnesota—where the Mayo Clinic is located—lies about 100 miles south of Minneapolis. It's a city with a population of 90,000, and it's surrounded by fields and farms. The two principal employers in Rochester are a huge IBM facility and, of course, the Mayo.

If you ever want to win a trivia contest, you can bring up the fact that Rochester has the smallest airport in the world that can accommodate a 747 jet. It has a landing strip that was built long enough to handle Air Force One and any other dignitary's wide-body jet.

You may remember a few years back when King Hussein of Jordan was commuting back and forth to the Mayo from Jordan. His Royal Jordanian DC10 flew directly into the tiny airport. Sadly, the king passed away from kidney cancer, but he left a legacy of kindness with the Mayo staff.

The Mayo Clinic is something to behold. The latest and greatest advancements in medicine normally go there first—if they haven't been researched there to begin with. The executive physical program is known throughout the world. When I went, there were people in the registration line from Argentina, France, Saudi Arabia, Japan, Germany and Brazil. I probably should have brought a soccer ball with me to entertain them all!

The Mayo Clinic has 28 full-time translators on staff to aid communication in every major language. The registration nurses are efficient and organized; the second I gave them my name, they handed me my two-and-a-half-day schedule with directions to each department because the clinic is spread out over five different buildings, with an underground walkway system connecting them all.

The registration nurse immediately asked me if I wanted to book my next physical for 2007 or 2008. I had not even started that one yet! She also explained to me that if I got lost or disoriented, I could come back to the desk and they would help me find my way. I started getting a bit nervous when she mentioned that.

The first order of business after registration was having blood drawn. I went to room 38 and checked in—with 96 other patients. I thought, *Oh my gosh, this is going to be a long wait.*

Wrong. There were 12 technicians drawing blood and I was out of there in 15 minutes. I could not believe how quickly they processed all of us. In my two and a half days there, I met with and was examined by 14 different doctors, scanned by 2 different machines and had the dreaded "you just turned 50 years old…time for the colonoscopy" treatment. Ouch!

The most amazing part about meeting 14 physicians was the consistency of their questions. First and foremost, whether a cardiologist or a dermatologist, each doctor asked, "Do you exercise? If so, how often and for how long?"

The next question was, "Do you eat a healthful diet with plenty of fruits and vegetables?" They all wrote the answers in my chart, which by the way was electronic. This was the Mayo, after all; I shouldn't have expected anything less than cutting-edge technology.

I finally had a chance to spend some time with the principal physician in charge of my case, Dr. John Hodgson. Having this book in mind, I wanted to ask him a lot of questions about the future of healthcare.

Dr. Hodgson was more than accommodating and thorough in answering all my questions. The first thing I asked him was why the constant questioning about exercise and diet?

He explained to me that the world of medicine and healthcare is changing. The most important thing anyone in the field of medicine can do now is evangelize about prevention, prevention and more prevention. In the world we Baby Boomers grew up in, the medical profession was all about diagnosis and treatment. We—and our doctors—knew very little about prevention.

Dr. Hodgson told me that 70 to 75 percent of all Boomer afflictions are preventable, or can at least be significantly delayed, with exercise and proper nutrition. Stop and think about that statement: 70 to 75 percent of all illnesses, diseases and general afflictions can be significantly delayed or prevented with a good exercise and nutrition program! Just think about how it could improve your quality of life as well.

With healthcare costs running so high, he said it was time for doctors and patients to invest in understanding what causes so many afflictions and to make sure we all have the tools for prevention. He went on to say that catching Boomers early, identifying their individual risks and immediately working on them would save our healthcare system billions and billions of dollars.

He said, "We no longer say 'You should lose weight' or 'You should quit smoking.' Instead it is, 'You **MUST** lose weight' or 'You **MUST** quit smoking.' This is followed by 'You **WILL** start an exercise program' and 'You **WILL** modify your diet.'" Wow…no more Dr. Nice Guy!

Hodgson and other physicians at the Mayo Clinic are dedicated to preventative medicine. High blood pressure, diabetes, high cholesterol and triglycerides, obesity, osteoporosis, joint pain and many other Baby Boomer afflictions are preventable or delayed by lifestyle changes and commitment to good health practices.

The cardiologist there explained to me that they are quicker now to prescribe blood pressure and cholesterol medications, even if the patient's levels are only borderline. High blood pressure and high cholesterol are two nasty, painless problems that build up over time and do damage to the circulatory system, so why not catch them early and slow them down or eradicate them with properly prescribed drugs?

If you ever have the opportunity to go through the Mayo executive physical or a similar program elsewhere, do it. I learned a lot about my own body and mortality, and how I can delay the onset of many of life's little nasties!

Looking to the Future of Healthcare

The pharmaceutical industry, including biotechnology companies and medical device sectors of the healthcare industry, will provide great innovation and excitement for us aging Boomers.

The major themes will include oncology (cancer) drugs, the treatment of HIV, hepatitis medications, ophthalmology (eye) care and disease prevention, and cardiovascular drugs. The medical devices industry will see improvements and new products in orthopedic care, including better prosthetic knees and hips.

Great advances are also being made in the treatment of spinal disorders and fractures. Young companies like Kyphon (KYPH) and old veterans like Medtronic (MDT) have been working on the next generation of spinal implants and devices that will help treat osteoporosis and other afflictions of the spinal column. Definitely an exciting new sector, employing minimally invasive surgical techniques as well.

A very important factor to consider with smaller and emerging medical device companies—and I will detail five of them in the stock recommendation section—is Medicare and general insurance reimbursement. Typically, insurance and Medicare play a little game of chicken to see which one flinches first. New medical devices not only have to prove their advantages over conventional treatment options, but they have to show reasonable cost as well.

Usually, insurers and Medicare listen to a groundswell of support and demand from doctors, as they are on the front lines with these new devices. Once either side flinches, the other tends to follow fairly quickly. Sometimes the reimbursement risk is priced into the stock's share price. The stock market doesn't appreciate devices that are out-of-pocket expenses for the patient because it is more difficult to model revenues and earnings consistently.

The following companies present interesting investment opportunities in the healthcare sector. You'll notice that I have not recommended any of the major pharmaceutical companies, *e.g.*, Merck, Pfizer, Johnson and Johnson or Bristol Myers Squibb, because that sector has been under pressure in 2006 and has yet to rebound.

However, 2007 and 2008 could be strong years for the major pharma companies as rotation begins back into the sector. Refer to my website for updates on the timeliness of these stocks.

Potential Booming Healthcare Stocks for Baby Boomers

Electro-Optical Sciences, Inc. (MELA)

MELA is developing and testing a new device to help more accurately detect melanomas, the most dangerous forms of skin cancer. The product, MelaFind, should have Food and Drug Administration (FDA) approval in early 2007, for a summer launch.

Currently, if a dermatologist suspects that a lesion may be cancerous, he or she must perform a painful and expensive biopsy. There are 2.5 million biopsies performed each year in the United States alone. Thankfully, more times than not, the lesions are non-cancerous. MelaFind will eliminate the guesswork in this process.

The market capitalization is only $61 million, but MELA should be a big winner. They need to train a sales force and put it in place, which takes time and money. MELA will not have any earnings until 2008 or 2009, but this is not an earnings story. Once the company receives final FDA approval, its stock will begin to run on the anticipation of earnings power and leverage. The end market is huge, and MELA should be the winner.

Genentech, Inc. (DNA)

Genentech's leadership in the oncology sector is monstrous and growing. DNA's portfolio of drugs includes those for the treatment of asthma, cystic fibrosis, hormone deficiency, plaque psoriasis and heart attack (point-of-attack clot-buster).

DNA has strong franchises with Rituxan, a treatment for rheumatoid arthritis, and Tarceva, a drug treatment for non-small cell lung cancer. Tarceva is also undergoing clinical trials for other indications including breast cancer treatment.

DNA is already an $83 billion market capitalization company, but it could become a $200 billion to $300 billion market capitalization stock over the next decade. It should hit revenues of $8.9 billion in 2006 and $11 billion in 2007, with earnings growing solidly at over 30 percent. Look for $2.05 in 2006 earnings per share and $2.65 to $2.70 in 2007.

Gilead Sciences, Inc. (GILD)

Gilead Sciences is the biopharmaceutical company leading the way in treating human immunodeficiency virus (HIV), the leading cause of AIDS. GILD has received approval for the launch of Atripla, a once-a-day pill for the treatment of HIV. This blockbuster could become a $2 billion product.

Gilead also manufactures Hepsera, which is used for the treatment of Hepatitis B. The company is the maker of Tamiflu for the treatment of influenza—a franchise that becomes even more valuable as the world braces for the potential of bird flu. All of these products are marketed worldwide

GILD has a $27 billion market capitalization and has a cash hoard of $3.3 billion, which will be used for strategic acquisitions. It has the potential to be a $100 billion market cap company over the next decade. This stock should be a core holding.

Kyphon, Inc. (KYPH)

Kyphon has FDA-approved products and tools for the treatment of spinal fractures normally caused by osteoporosis. There are about 700,000 vertebral compression fractures each year in the United States that require surgery to repair; in response, Kyphon has developed minimally invasive surgical tools and "bone cement" that is employed to fill gaps between the vertebrae, to cure the fracture.

Osteoporosis affects mostly women, and as the population ages, there will be a bigger patient population for Kyphon's products

KYPH has a market capitalization of $1.4 billion and its revenue run rate is approaching $400 million. The operating margin is about 16 percent and going higher. It has no reimbursement issues and it has the biggest sales force in the spinal sector.

KYPH will face competition from Medtronic (MDT) but should continue to dominate because it owns the doctor relationships and the market is big enough for two or three players. KYPH could be an acquisition target in the next one to four years.

NuVasive, Inc. (NUVA)

NuVasive is a leader in a vast array of spinal surgical products to help treat disc and nerve problems. The company has an application at the FDA for an artificial disc, which would address a large market.

NUVA has a market capitalization of $600 million and revenues should approach $100 million in 2007. Earnings will turn positive in late 2007 and should accelerate from there. NUVA plays in the $5 billion spinal surgical products market, but that market is growing by 20 percent every year. NUVA is establishing a formidable sales force and the leverage will become apparent in 2007.

St. Jude Medical, Inc. (STJ)

St. Jude is one of the leading cardiovascular companies in the world. It has many products for the cardiac care industry including pacemakers, implantable defibrillators and surgery tools, and it is the leader in cardiac tissue valves and mechanical valves. Its distribution power is worldwide.

As Boomers age, cardiac devices will be more and more in demand. St. Jude could accelerate its growth over the next one to three years because it is pioneering a device for atrial fibrillation, the most common cardiac arrhythmia.

The important issue to keep focused on is Medicare reimbursement. Medicare is usually quite compliant with St. Jude, Medtronic and Boston Scientific, allowing for 3 to 5 percent price increases every year. St. Jude has a market capitalization of $11.5 billion and 2006 revenues in excess of $3.3 billion. STJ is one to own for one to three years at least.

Zimmer Holdings, Inc. (ZMH)

Zimmer is one of the three big companies that address the orthopedic market. The other two are Biomet (BMET) and Stryker Corp. (SYK). Zimmer has a broader product set than the other two because it offers major dental devices and spinal products as well as the orthopedic products.

Zimmer has pioneered and trained several thousand orthopedic surgeons in minimally invasive surgical techniques. The company—as well as its two competitors—are at the low end of their 52-week stock prices. The reason is that there may be indictments of some surgeons and orthopedic executives by the U.S. Justice Department. The government feels that these companies employ too many surgeons as "consultants" and give them lucrative deals which give the impression of being kickbacks.

Whatever the outcome, the orthopedic space is growing by leaps and bounds as Baby Boomers are aging and developing creaky elbows, knees, hips and shoulders.

ZMH is positioned for terrific growth. Currently, it has a $16.2 billion market capitalization, and revenues should hit $3.55 billion in 2006 and approach $4 billion in 2007. Its operating profit margin is around 30-plus percent.

SYK and BMET should follow ZMH's stock performance, but ZMH will outpace them. When the Justice Department probe clears up—and there may be some significant fines or even imprisonments—the cloud will come off the group. Whatever the outcome, the sector is still vital and growing strongly.

For continuous updates on the performance of these stocks, specific recommendations, initial price targets, earnings and revenue discussion, growth rates, competitive positioning, addressable market size and general market commentary, please refer to my website, www.investingbabyboomer.com.

CHAPTER FOUR

LIFESTYLE: WHAT'S YOUR E-MAIL ADDRESS?

"HEY, GOOD BUDDY, WHAT'S YOUR HANDLE?"

"Breaker, breaker, my handle is Frenchy Wheels. What's your handle, good buddy?"

Remember the citizens' band radio, otherwise known as the CB? What was once the communication tool of choice for truck drivers became a popular consumer toy because of Congress' implementation and strict enforcement of the nationwide, 55 mile per hour speed limit in 1974. We all knew where "Smokey" was hiding and where the speed traps were laid out. It was a ton of fun to think of a "handle" and speak the lingo.

It was the first time most motorists had any kind of external communication device. We could actually talk to people— or "good buddies"—within a range of a couple miles. It was a great toy for most of us, and in my case, it kept me from a few speeding tickets.

The culmination of the CB craze came in 1977, with the release of a very popular movie called *Smokey and the Bandit*, starring Burt Reynolds, Sally Fields and Jackie Gleason.

Lifestyles, They Are A-Changin'

Baby Boomers have seen the most advances and technological developments in comfort, communication and consumer choices than any other generation. But, our children and grandchildren will, of course, see more in their lifetimes.

Think back, Boomer, to when you were a kid, whether you were raised in the country, in a small town or in a big city. Back then, we didn't really have a lot of choices as consumers. Our parents and grandparents typically shopped at the local grocery store, the local drugstore (which also had an ice cream fountain), the local hardware store and the local family clothing store.

Now we find it "charming" when we discover a Mom-and-Pop store. The big national names back in the 1950s and 60s were Woolworth's, Sears (where America shopped) and Montgomery Ward's. Notice how two of the three are completely gone—and the remainder, Sears, has finally been reinvented, or it too would have hit the ash heap.

We grew up with the idea that we should "build and buy American." We had to keep Americans employed at all costs. Our parents and grandparents survived the Great Depression and knew the value of a dollar and the importance of keeping jobs intact. They did not mind the competition between Chrysler, General Motors, Ford and American Motors, as all were American made and serviced.

When the "imports" began to arrive on our shores in the late 1960s, we began to realize that German and Japanese cars actually offered better quality and workmanship. I remember how many of my parents' friends were horrified when my father bought a 1968 Mercedes sedan—that is, until they rode in it or drove it. Then, the scowls turned to smiles and admiration of the vehicle's quality.

We began to buy Japanese, German and Swedish cars with greater ease, and we had to add new names to our vocabulary: BMW, Audi, Saab, Volvo, Mercedes-Benz. Unfortunately, we also got to delete a few names from our vocabulary, such as American Motors and its Rambler, Javelin and Ambassador models.

In 1980, the U.S. government put together a financial package that saved Chrysler Corporation from bankruptcy, and we began to see the CEO emerge as a celebrity. Remember Lee Iacocca? Seems like yesterday, doesn't it?

A shocking statistic today: the *combined* market capitalization value of General Motors (GM) and Ford Motors (F) is $31 billion. The same value of Toyota Motors (TM) is $175 billion, or 5.5 times larger. The investing world has voted, and Toyota is the winner by a landslide.

In the 1970s and 80s, we became more comfortable with buying foreign consumer goods like cameras, clothes and televisions and other electronics. "Made in Japan" no longer carried the "cheaply made" connotation from the 50s and 60s. Instead, it began to represent quality and verifiable competition.

Little did we Baby Boomers know it at the time, but we were creating and embracing the global economy. International competition forced American businesses to become leaner in their operations; they actually had to formulate three to five-year business plans and understand that their products could also play in the world's market.

Some of the disasters of the past 30 years include Wang Laboratories, Digital Equipment Corp. and Control Data Corp. They just couldn't keep up with the global changes and rising expectations that competition fostered.

Competition Branches Out

The 1970s and 80s began a period when the consumer became more informed and much choosier. In the late 70s, Wal-Mart began to flourish in our country and it set the stage for other retailers to think nationally, not just locally or regionally. A war arose between Kmart and Wal-Mart, and the winner was the consumer; some would say Kmart was the loser in this battle.

We had more and better choices at lower prices. Target stores began to expand from their Midwest base and now are a national player, putting the pressure on Wal-Mart. Mom-and-Pop stereo stores began to face huge pricing and choice pressures from the emergence of Best Buy Corp. and Circuit City. Both began to dominate the electronics retail distribution in the 80s and 90s and have been two of the better performing stocks of the past 25 years.

American consumers, led by us Baby Boomers, started to crave better and more creative choices for dining out. Working couples became more common and therefore eating at home became less and less frequent.

The 1970s, 80s and 90s brought us a whole group of restaurant concepts: Houlihan's, Applebee's, Outback Steakhouse, Boston Market, Lone Star Steakhouse and Saloon, Macaroni Grill, Chili's, Red Lobster, Pizza Hut, Papa John's and many, many more. The upscale chains include Ruth's Chris Steak House, Capital Grille and Morton's Steakhouse, to name a few.

The multi-unit restaurant concept brought consistency of taste, service and décor. As one of my British clients so aptly noted, "It's the neonization of America." I confessed that I did not understand, so he went on to explain that "no matter what city or town you visit in America, there are always two or three streets that are full of the same neon lights from the same restaurants." He is right.

The restaurant stocks, almost each and every one of them, have had their days in the sun. They tend to be better for trading than buy-and-hold stocks for several reasons, including the one factor analysts cannot put into their financial models: the weather, which does to a certain degree dictate traffic flow.

The other factor that most analysts miss is what I affectionately call "menu fatigue." After a while, a concept just gets tiring and boring, and there are only so many ways to cook a chicken!

Two exciting concepts that I believe will hold consumers' attention for a number of years are California Pizza Kitchen (CPKI) and Chipotle Mexican Grill (CMG). Both offer fresh ingredients, which are becoming more important as we embrace healthier eating habits, and both have room for hundreds and hundreds of new units before they hit saturation and begin to see unit dollar volumes decrease. More on these two stocks later.

The changes and enhancements American consumers have enjoyed over the last 25 years have all come down to visionary entrepreneurs implementing focused concepts, and then executing them better than anyone else. Think about the ideas and concepts that have been born and raised in that time: Home Depot, Lowe's, Ace Hardware, Bed Bath and Beyond, Linens 'n Things, Costco, Staples, Office Max, Borders, Barnes and Noble, Dick's Sporting Goods, Target and many more.

These retail concepts were brilliant for consumers because they gave great choices, great quality and the best prices, but they were also brilliant for their shareholders. Huge wealth has been created with these retail concepts. Collectively, these publicly traded retail concepts represent hundreds of billions of dollars of created wealth and shareholder value.

Out With the Old, In With the New

I have saved the best for last: Starbucks Corp. (SBUX). In *Stop Losing Money Today*, I stated that I believe Starbucks will become bigger than McDonald's. Well, as of this writing, McDonald's (MCD) has a market capitalization of $41 billion and Starbucks' is $23 billion.

McDonald's went public with its initial public offering (IPO) in 1965; Starbucks' IPO was in 1992. In the 1950s, 60s and 70s, McDonald's changed Americans' eating habits and lead them to accept the concept of "fast food." Driving through, eating on the run, carrying it out—McDonald's changed the dining behavior of an entire nation.

The concept has been imitated by many since, like Burger King, Sonic, Taco Bell, KFC and Jack in the Box. But, pardon the pun, McDonald's set the table. They got into the head and the psyche of every little kid with the Happy Meal, which has a free toy inside and is emblazoned with the Ronald McDonald character.

By any measure, it's brilliant marketing, as McDonald's realized early on that kids have a big influence on where the family goes to eat. When's the last time you heard a four-year-old say, "Mommy, Daddy, let's go to Applebee's"?

McDonald's currently has 30,000 units in 119 countries; it's just an amazing success story. Yet, I would not buy the stock. Why? Its better days are behind it, and it is facing constant nutritional battles, menu experimentation and better competition than it was used to facing earlier in its history. The bad press from the documentary movie *Super Size Me* didn't help its public relations effort. (With all that said, I still have a weakness for their French fries!)

Again, I think that Starbucks will be bigger and better than

McDonald's. Since its IPO, Starbucks has already attained a $23 billion market value. I believe that it will be a $100 billion market capitalization stock in the next five to seven years. The company's execution has been flawless, the consistency of each unit is near perfection and its commitment to a quality product is second to none.

Starbucks will also emerge as one of the world's biggest sellers of music and movies. What? Am I kidding? No, I'm not. Starbucks selectively places cool, nostalgic music CDs in its stores, and it features one artist a day. Whether it is the best of Ella Fitzgerald, Nat King Cole or Tony Bennett, it's the music you would not normally rush out to buy at a music store. It is purely an impulse buy and a stroke of marketing genius. Starbucks will begin that same approach to movies in DVD format.

The company has also successfully launched a "Starbucks card" on which patrons typically buy up to $25 of credit to use when buying their coffee and other products. When the card runs out of credit, the patron re-ups with another dollar amount. This system captures customers and builds their loyalty. As another way to capture and keep the customer, Starbucks offers wireless Internet connectivity in most of its stores.

In addition, Starbucks will be the largest coffee vendor in China. It will build more than 10,000 units in that country over the next decade. There are no other coffee players trying to capture the massive Chinese market.

Currently, Starbucks has 11,500 units worldwide. Like McDonald's, it has its share of competitors, like Caribou (CBOU), Cosi (COSI) and Peet's (PEET), but none of these will touch Starbucks' scale and worldwide presence.

Digital Cameras, Electronic Résumés and Paperless Checks

Technological advances of the past 25 years, particularly the Internet, have not only created massive new industries—for example, online education, online travel services and online poker—but have made our lives more challenging.

Remember when you bought that first camera, put in your Kodak film, took your pictures and then took them to the photo shop for development? Sometimes it took a couple of days to get your photos back, and then you had to accept what you received. Or maybe you were slick and used a Polaroid and had that photo in two or three minutes. The quality was suspect, but the gratification was instant.

Well, Polaroid, which used to be a stock market nifty-fifty, is gone as we know it, bought out by a private equity company. And Kodak has had to reinvent itself into a more diversified company.

Digital photography is now the norm. The quality of the photo is spectacular and the photographer can delete unwanted shots immediately. The price of a good quality digital camera has come down to $250 to $300. We can put the photos on a CD, download them onto our PCs and then e-mail them to whomever across the world—all in about five minutes. Just think about that: could you have imagined this elaborate process even 10 years ago?

Funny story: at my eldest daughter Stephanie's wedding in 2005, at the end of the reception, I asked the photographer how many pictures he had taken throughout the day. I was stunned when she casually replied, "About 2,000."

I screamed, "Two thousand! Where's all your film?"

She coolly replied, "It's digital, baby. I don't do film!"

My daughter told me to take a breath and relax. "Welcome to the 2000s, Dad!" she said.

Remember how it used to be when you were applying for a job? You put together a résumé and mailed it out or dropped it off to several potential employers, and then you waited for the phone to ring. The process took several days to several weeks.

Now, we go online and list our résumé on Monster.com (MNST) and save the postage! Monster.com has redefined the way to get a job, whether locally or across the country. Employers are very comfortable with the Website's reliability and quality control. Monster.com is now a $5 billion market capitalization company doing $1 billion in annual revenues, and it has about a 20 percent operating profit margin.

Maybe you are one of the 18 million American consumers who receives, reviews and pays your regular monthly bills online. Bank of America has been the pioneer and leading force in this convenience. Other major financial institutions offer the service as well.

The company that dominates the technology behind the scenes and makes it a seamless service for the bank is CheckFree Corp. (CKFR). This is a $3.2 billion market capitalization company approaching $1 billion in revenues, and it is very profitable.

Why do banks offer this service free of charge when for them, it's costly? Simple—once you have bill review and payment through a bank, chances are very high that you will remain with that bank and consume or buy other products like a mortgage, retirement account or savings account. It's a win-win situation for the consumer, the bank and the dominant player working behind the scenes, CheckFree Corp.

Virtual Home Buying

Buying and selling real estate has almost become a sport in the United States. In the old days—meaning about six or seven years ago—we would phone a Realtor, make an appointment and begin to scour the newspaper ads and go to the open houses.

Not anymore. With companies like Move, Inc. (MOVE) (name changed in June 2006; formerly known as Homestore), the process of assessing real estate has become fairly simple. On its Website, Move.com, this company has amalgamated the 2.1 million listings across the United States and divided them up by ZIP code and market value.

Many Realtors have their Websites on Move.com. Whether you are looking to move to another city or just three blocks down the street, once you put in that location's ZIP code, you'll get a local Realtor's Website as well as the listings in that zip code by price range.

Move earns its revenues by charging the Realtors for the Websites, and it sells advertising on the main Move, Inc. Website to mortgage, moving and insurance companies. It's a great model and Move, Inc. could become the dominant player in the sector.

Move maintains that 72 percent of all real estate searches begin on the Internet, and yet only 4 to 5 percent of the advertising and marketing budgets are spent online. There is a strong disconnect here; Move contends, and I agree, that more advertising/marketing dollars should go to the online sites.

Personal Computing Power

Baby Boomers, could we exist without a personal computer (PC)? Whether it is a laptop or a desktop unit, life would be very complicated without one. Funny, my kids remind me that getting the first home computer complicated my life because I had to learn how to use it! Now, life would be extremely complicated without it! Go figure.

For the 2006 school year, my two younger children are receiving laptops from their school; each student will be issued one, from fourth to twelfth grade. My daughter Alexandra is a junior and my son Joseph is an eighth grader. Both will be expected to use these computers to take notes, do homework assignments, research various science and history projects and write all their papers. Of course, both have school-issued email addresses as well.

How did we Baby Boomers get through high school and college without these amenities?! Even 10 short years ago it was rare to have a personal e-mail address. In 1996, businesses were putting e-mail systems into use, but consumer adoption was in its infancy.

Now, when people meet for the first time, rather than exchanging phone numbers, they exchange e-mail addresses. When I buy something from any retailer, in person or online, one of the first questions asked is "What is your e-mail address?" Once you give it up, retailers will ping you with information about your purchase and of course inform you when they have a sale going on. Appliance vendors want your e-mail address to keep you informed about warranty expiration and to "offer" you the chance to extend it.

Walgreens informs me that my prescription is ready for renewal…via e-mail. Blockbuster reminds me to please bring back the movies I rented…via e-mail. The airlines remind me of my flight tomorrow and allow me to print up my boarding pass at home…both via e-mail.

E-mail brings me the news that my bank has a new mortgage program or an interest rate change; it even reminds me when I have to go for my six-month dental checkup. In addition, the veterinarian e-mails me every month to see how my family's dogs are feeling (though I'm not sure how to ask my dogs such a personal question.)

The worldwide e-mail system is the cheapest way to advertise, market and stay in touch with your customers and prospects. According to the U.S. Department of Trade and Industry, there are 50 billion e-mails sent every day worldwide—up from 12 billion per day in 2001—and 88 percent of them are considered junk mail.

A person receives 32 e-mails per day on average, up 84 percent year over year, and there are currently 440 million e-mail addresses worldwide. These are stunning numbers, and they are growing.

Instant Gratification on the Internet

The Internet has radically changed our lives—period. It's the greatest discovery and achievement since a) the wheel, b) electricity or c) *Desperate Housewives*! Whichever you pick for comparison, the magnitude of the Internet is almost immeasurable.

The Internet service providers, search engine companies and major retailers have created well over $1 trillion of shareholder value—that's ONE TRILLION—all within the last 10 to 12 years.

Amazon.com (AMZN) was formed in 1995 and went public in 1997, and it has a market capitalization of $11.1 billion. Another product of 1995 was eBay (EBAY), which went public in 1997 and is now worth a market capitalization of $34 billion. Both Google and Yahoo opened their doors in the mid-90s and since going public have created a combined $150 billion of market capitalization.

The Internet has served to keep us informed with news of the world transmitted in seconds. Blogs—a new word in our vocabulary—allow us to comment on any situation or event instantly. Anyone can create a new blog for virtually no cost and build a community of like-minded thinkers—or detractors.

The Internet has given us Boomers the ability to be vocal and opinionated, yet remain anonymous by using creative screen names. There are also many chat rooms where we can exchange anything from recipes to pregnancy information to movie reviews.

On the Internet, political and economic news can be quickly commented on by both sides of the aisle. Some will say that Dan Rather of CBS News was brought to task by the blogging community when a suspect report about President Bush's military service came into question, just before the November 2004 election.

Bloggers immediately challenged the authenticity of the documents CBS News was basing its report on. It really demonstrated the first time that the blogger community successfully challenged the credibility of a major news agency—*and won.*

The Baby Boomer generation is comfortable with shopping online. Look at the businesses that have been created these past 10 years, including names like Expedia and Priceline.com for travel services. We can take a virtual tour of almost any destination before committing to an airline ticket.

Amazon.com and BarnesandNoble.com have built sustainable businesses selling books, movies and music CDs. Online auctioning is now practically a cyber sport, thanks to eBay; I know several people who actually make their livings buying and selling items on that site alone. Imagine putting that as job experience on your résumé!

Several existing retailers, with successful bricks-and-mortar business models, have enhanced their businesses by building excellent websites and allowing for online transactions. Check out the Websites for Wal-Mart, Target and Costco: they're allowing for significant add-on sales, as foot traffic to these retailers has not been reduced by their online presences.

The Internet is also the new public library. We Boomers have queried Google and other search engines billions of times. Our children and grandchildren are more encouraged to search online than to learn how to navigate a library. My eighth and eleventh graders do all their research and inquiries on the Internet.

Many educators have argued that searching online enables students to learn more about a subject because the information and the subcategories appear quicker and in a much better organized fashion, thus allowing students to "absorb" more. Unfortunately, listening to your child taking tuba lessons is still a real-world experience!

Learn It All Online

One industry that has helped millions of Baby Boomers and their children is online education. These Internet schools offer degree certification in business, nursing, engineering and many other disciplines. Through these businesses, many adults have been granted the opportunity to complete or extend their educations for job promotions or changes.

The pioneer company in the industry has been Apollo Group, Inc. (APOL) and its key subsidiary, The University of Phoenix online. There are some physical campuses, but the bulk of the business is on the Internet. The student population is not only American, but international as well.

Apollo Group, Inc. has had some recent execution issues, but it's still considered the leader and has a $7.7 billion market capitalization, generating revenues of about $2.5 billion, with operating margins approaching 30 percent.

Another emerging company in the sector is Corinthian Colleges, Inc. (COCO), which offers degrees in information technology, healthcare and business. It also offers certification in several mechanical disciplines such as automotive, aircraft, marine and motorcycle. COCO has a market capitalization of $1.1 billion and revenues of about $1.0 billion.

Another interesting company that has experienced some execution issues is Educate, Inc. (EEEE). This company operates and franchises out over 1,100 Sylvan Learning Centers. It has a well-known brand name and specializes in helping grade school and high school students. The market capitalization is about $270 million, and its revenue run rate is about $300 million as well.

Educate, Inc. is struggling with profitability. If it executes its business plan properly, the stock will be inexpensive; otherwise, it will be taken over by a larger player because the Sylvan brand is worth a lot in the marketplace. This industry is just getting its feet wet and the future offerings will be even more sophisticated and complete.

The Boomer lifestyle and the changes we've experienced these past 30 years could fill volumes. From organic food and natural, homeopathic treatments, to state-of-the-art exercise equipment (with personal trainers, of course) and the sophistication of our PCs, cell phones and HDTVs, to the intricacies of the Internet, we will strive for more and better mousetraps.

Listed below are companies that continue to enhance our lives, as well as emerging companies that will add even more to the aforementioned. Enjoy, and good investing.

Potential Booming Lifestyle
Stocks for Baby Boomers

Audible, Inc. (ADBL)

Audible markets audio entertainment as well as educational and informational programming on the Internet, in formats that are downloadable to an MP3 player or iPod.

Consumers who desire daily news, sports and business stories from several national newspapers can download them overnight from Audible for a monthly subscription fee. Consumers can also subscribe to weekly periodicals and easily download books.

Audible sells various programming *á la carte* and has an excellent relationship with Apple Computer's iPod division, in which Apple co-markets for ADBL for first-time iPod buyers. Audible is making serious inroads into the educational space, where college students will soon be able to download textbooks right onto their MP3 players. Pearson, the largest marketers of college textbooks, is working with Audible on this opportunity.

ADBL has had some execution issues over the past two or three years, but it appears positioned to consistently grow both revenues and earnings. The Street measures Audible's quarterly success on new net subscriber growth and the cost of acquiring a new subscriber.

Audible has the early mover advantage over its competition, and with its premier status with Apple's iPod, this $175 million market capitalization company could be a 3 to 4-bagger over the next few years.

Bright Horizons Family Solutions, Inc. (BFAM)

Bright Horizons operates 611 childcare centers, currently serving about 67,000 children. BFAM markets to the Fortune 500 to feature childcare as an employee benefit. Currently, 80 companies of the Fortune 500 employ BFAM's services.

As employment in the United States holds firm, childcare is becoming a critical benefit to employees. With BFAM's blue-chip client list, its marketing efforts give it a terrific advantage over its competition. BFAM has excellent management; the original founders still run the company.

BFAM is a terrific story of solid cash-flow generation and 25-plus percent earnings and revenue growth. It currently has a market capitalization of $1.1 billion, with 2006 revenues of $705 million and 2007 expectations of $825 million; earnings for 2006 are $1.48 per share and expected 2007 earnings are $1.80 per share. Stock could be a 4 to 5-bagger over the next 5 years. Great story with rising margins and great cash-flow generation.

California Pizza Kitchen, Inc. (CPKI)

California Pizza Kitchen operates 193 stores in the United States. Of those, 161 are company-owned and 32 are franchise operations. CPKI runs about a $13 average check per customer.

The company uses the freshest of ingredients for their meal-sized salads and their personalized pizzas—customers can order from a range of pizza selections or design their own. Superb execution has been CPKI's hallmark. It has room to more than double its current restaurant base, and its growth rate has been a solid 25 percent.

Current market capitalization is $550 million, with room to triple the stock over the next three years. Excellent management team and a fresh, creative menu.

Chipotle Mexican Grill, Inc. (CMG)

The founding and financing of the Chipotle concept was helped along by McDonald's, although the involvement is currently ending as the latter corporation sells its remaining shares.

CMG has over 500 units, with room to triple that amount to 1,500. Its terrific menu features fresh ingredients and made-to-order food, and in addition to their in-house service, they run a great carryout business as well. Some feel that CMG is expensive, but monthly same-store sales have seen double-digit increases. Repeat customer traffic is huge, although CMG has not stated the actual percentage of repeat customers.

Chipotle has a current market capitalization of $1.6 billion. Revenue growth is a solid 25 to 30 percent, expecting $800 million for 2006 and $1 billion for 2007. Earnings are expected to be $0.88 per share for 2006 and $1.10 for 2007.

CMG has a chance to be the dominant Mexican restaurant concept in the United States and Canada. The company is very well capitalized and financed and should emerge as one of the premier stocks in the restaurant sector. Stock should double to triple over the next three to five years.

Corinthian Colleges, Inc. (COCO)

COCO offers diplomas in associate, bachelor and master degree programs, with specialties in healthcare, business, technology and criminal justice. The student body is now over 70,000, spread over 131 schools in 25 states.

COCO is picking up momentum—new management has made significant strides to gain accreditation for all its different schools. It has been marketing successfully, as student body count has been increasing.

COCO is a $1.1 billion market capitalization company with revenues just topping $1 billion. Earnings are expected to be $0.57 for calendar year 2006 and $0.70 to $0.73 for 2007. COCO needs to execute its plan to drive higher margins and better profitability. This could be a 2 to 3-bagger over the next 2 or 3 years.

Costco Wholesale Corp. (COST)

Costco operates membership-based warehouses that offer consumers both branded products and goods from its signature in-house private brand, Kirkland. Costco is spread out over 471 units worldwide—346 in the U.S. and the rest in Canada, the United Kingdom, Taiwan, Japan and Mexico.

Products range from fresh produce to toiletries, electronics, home furnishings, and much more. The memberships are tiered from business to consumer. Costco has had tremendous success in beating Sam's Club of Wal-Mart in head-to-head competition—in monthly same-store sales, they've topped them in 47 out of 48 months.

COST is currently a $24 billion market capitalization company with the opportunity to be $100 billion to $150 billion. It has begun a share buyback program, as its cash and current assets position is north of $8 billion.

The one concern I have is that COST is so cash rich and cash-flow positive that it makes an attractive acquisition candidate for a Berkshire Hathaway-type suitor. I hope this concept is allowed to play its hand over the next 5 to 10 years as a public company, because it could be a huge winner.

Dick's Sporting Goods, Inc. (DKS)

Dick's has emerged as the premier sporting goods retailer in the United States. Currently, DKS operates 263 stores in the country, with the capacity to double that amount over the next 5 to 7 years.

DKS has executed its plan superbly where others have failed. Their stores offer sports apparel, exercise and fitness equipment, and a variety of golf, tennis, baseball, football and other sports equipment. The company is renowned for having a very knowledgeable staff at the store level, which helps make the consumer shopping experience pleasant and rewarding.

Dick's has a loyalty club that rewards its customers with discounts and free items when certain dollar amounts are spent. It also has an enviable 5 to 6 percent operating margin, which is on the high end for a retail concept. This $1.9 billion market capitalization company could triple its value over the next 5 years.

Electronic Arts, Inc. (ERTS)

ERTS has the brand names of EA Games, EA Sports and EA Sports Big. Its Madden Football series of video games is probably one of its most popular and well-known products.

ERTS is a $14 billion market capitalization company that could double in the next 2 to 3 years. The company has had relatively flat revenues the past 3 years—around $3 billion—but has increased its research and development spending by $258 million, up to $758 million.

Due to the flat revenues and increased research and development spending, ERTS has sacrificed its near-term earnings these past 2 years, but it will lead the pack with newer and better games in late 2006, and it is embarking on an aggressive program of wireless games. As this channel becomes bigger, ERTS will once again experience growth in the 20-plus percent range for both revenues and earnings.

Google, Inc. (GOOG)

The Google search engine is the envy of all competitors, and the investment company has made and continues to make in its product is unparalleled. Google is capturing market share in the online marketing and advertising world, and it will emerge as the number one or two player in the space.

Google has many product offerings for its customers, including Froogle shopping services, map searches, scholar search services, Google news—and the list goes on.

The company has acquired a market capitalization of $112 billion in less than 2 years. Unbelievable and stunning, yet this company has its better days yet to come. Wall Street analysts have had to adjust their revenue and earnings estimates upward virtually every quarter since the company went public.

Currently, estimates call for revenues of $6.9 billion for 2006 and $9.9 billion for 2007, with earnings for 2006 at $10.20 per share and for 2007 at $13.25 per share. They will probably be adjusted higher again.

I have been asked so many times who is the next Microsoft or Cisco, and I always answer that it's Google—except Google will probably become bigger than both of them. This could become a $500 billion market capitalization company in 3 to 5 years. The story and the fundamentals are that compelling. Google should be a core holding.

Intuit, Inc. (INTU)

Intuit makes financial management software for the small business, professional accountant and consumer markets. TurboTax and QuickBooks are their two most popular product lines.

INTU markets its products through a direct sales force, retail stores and the exciting and growing channel of its Website. The site is easy to navigate and buy from and will lift the company's margins even higher than they are at present.

Intuit holds more than 70 percent market share in the small business/consumer financial software market. It will easily protect and grow the market share with its Website innovations.

The company's business is very seasonal, to the point where it actually loses money in quarters ending July 31 and October 31. However, the profits of the quarters ending January 31 and April 30 are absolutely huge and more than make up for the other two poor ones.

INTU has a market capitalization of $10.7 billion with a revenue run rate of $2.5 billion, and earnings of over $2.80 per share for fiscal year July 2007. Operating margins run in the 28 to 29 percent range, with room to go higher. It could become a $25 billion to $30 billion market capitalization company over the next 2 to 4 years. Great story, solid franchise.

Move, Inc. (MOVE)

Move, Inc. was previously known as Homestore but changed its corporate name to avoid confusion with home furnishings makers. Move has an excellent website, Move.com, which amalgamates the 2.1 million homes and condominiums for sale in the United States at any given time.

Real estate agents will pay Move to create a Website on their behalf to help attract buyers and sellers and to market their services to their local community. As mentioned earlier, although 72 percent of all real estate inquiries begin online, only 4 to 5 percent of the advertising and marketing budgets are spent there.

Move maintains that the spending habits of marketers will shift even more to the Internet channel, and it stands as the potential dominant player in this space.

Current market capitalization is $580 million, and 2006 revenues should be $290 million, growing to $350 million to $360 million in 2007. MOVE is breaking even in 2006 earnings and should earn between $0.21 and $0.25 per share in 2007.

The stock is cheap as far as market cap to revenue ratio is concerned. If MOVE executes cleanly, this stock could be a three to five-bagger over the next three to five years. The leverage in the model could be dramatic. Slowing real estate values should not affect MOVE because realtors will spend more to advertise and market their properties.

Napster, Inc. (NAPS)

Napster is anything but napping! This company provides online music for the consumer market, and its audience is worldwide. NAPS has a subscription-based model whereby its customers can choose from over two million songs in the company's library and download them to their personal computers.

Napster allows its customers to share songs and search each other's collections. The company also sells individual songs for non-subscribers. This company has seeded the marketplace and has strategic relationships with Dell, Samsung, Gateway, Toshiba, Best Buy, Tower Records and The Dixon Group, where NAPS is featured as a preferred partner.

NAPS recently signed an agreement with NTT DoCoMo of Japan, which has the biggest network of wireless customers—about 48 million. The company is also making inroads into the wireless world, which will exponentially expand its addressable market.

Although NAPS has a lot of work and execution in front of it, the risk/reward here is appetizing. It has a market capitalization of only $125 million—more than half of which is in cash—and has been running sizable losses. The company should turn profitable in calendar 2008. It is also a very good takeover candidate for a larger company.

Starbucks, Inc. (SBUX)

I discussed Starbucks at length earlier in this chapter, but I want to reiterate how important this concept and company is, and the potential that lies in front of it.

Currently, SBUX has 11,500 units in its system, with the potential for 30,000 to 35,000 units worldwide. The company is creating new drinks besides its vast choices of coffee, and it will be a major marketer of music CDs and movie DVDs. SBUX is passionate about store-level execution, where it has excelled.

With a current market capitalization of $23 billion, it has both the opportunity and the potential to be a $100 billion market capitalization company. Earnings should sustain at a 20 percent growth clip for the next 3 to 5 years.

Whole Foods Market, Inc. (WFMI)

Whole Foods operates 171 natural and organic food supermarkets and it has expanded its brand to include pet products, floral arrangements and household cleaning products. With the U.S. consumer trending more and more to organic, pest-control-free food products, WFMI is emerging as the leading player in the space.

The company has room to double its store base in the United States and continue to expand in the United Kingdom and Canada. Typically, organic food is more expensive, but WFMI is able to buy in bulk and keep its pricing more than competitive.

The current market capitalization is $7.2 billion, with revenues approaching $5 billion. The company has an excellent operating margin of nearly 5 percent. Stock should be considered a core holding.

Yahoo! Inc. (YHOO)

YHOO provides Internet services to consumers and businesses worldwide. It offers search engine capabilities, shopping online, email services, maps, auto shopping, financial information and about 50 other services.

Yahoo! is capturing more Internet advertising and marketing budgets as this phenomenon continues to evolve away from television, radio and print. This company is one of the main winners, along with its chief competitor, Google.

In the future, the Yahoo! model will migrate toward more

wireless services. Although it has not captured the sizzle that Google has in the stock market—Yahoo's growth has been less than Google's—the market has overdone its value compression on the company.

This $38 billion market capitalization company is less than 12 years old. Yahoo! will do revenues of $5 billion in 2006 and $6 billion in 2007, with operating margins north of 20 percent; earnings are $0.50 per share for 2006 and $0.70 per share for 2007. YHOO should be a core holding for the next 3 to 5 years, at least.

Youbet.com (UBET)

Youbet is a leading provider of online wagering services for horseracing. Its portfolio includes quarter horse, harness and thoroughbred racing.

UBET is licensed in 41 states to promote advanced deposit wagering (ADW), whereby a customer deposits funds with UBET and uses the account in picking races. Winnings are then credited to the account.

Youbet provides great service to its customers, as its Website streams over 60,000 hours of various races per week. This allows its customers to watch the races in real time. The Kentucky Derby is included in this racing stable (pardon the pun), and UBET is the exclusive provider of horseracing content to CBS SportsLine.com. UBET is also testing a wireless system and service, which will allow for nice customer growth.

UBET has a market capitalization of only $125 million, with a revenue run rate of $150 million, and it is profitable. Earnings per share in 2006 should be $0.27 and should be $0.40 to $0.42 in 2007. This is a very cheap valuation for a large, emerging player in the sector, and UBET has international presence and will grow through organic means and timely acquisitions. This stock could be a 5 to 10-bagger over the next 3 to 5 years.

For more stock ideas and greater details about the above-mentioned companies, please come to my Website, www.investingbabyboomer.com.

CHAPTER FIVE

TECHNOLOGY AND COMMUNICATIONS: CHANGE IS A-COMIN'

THERE IS NO QUESTION THAT WE HAVE WITNESSED a technology and communications boom in these past 33 years. To detail it would require 5 books, and I would still miss half of the accomplishments that mankind has achieved.

But look at our everyday existence: how many times are we enjoying the conveniences of technology? We so take it for granted these days that we wonder how we ever got along without it. Technology advances have increased the most important contributor to overall economic growth—productivity.

Saving Time: Faxes, E-mails and Cell Phones

From the late 1980s to 2001, corporations (private and public) and governments (state, local and federal) embarked on a capital spending spree that we never experienced before. Buying the best and latest technology became critical to modernizing systems and making certain that all systems were "talking" to each other via software and hardware.

"Enterprise software" became a new expression in our

vocabulary. Use of the local area network (LAN) became mission critical to enterprises, letting computers communicate with each other within a company. Then came the advent of the wide area network (WAN), allowing branch offices and remote locations of a company to be in the loop and communicate with each other as well as with company headquarters.

Both LAN and WAN became synonymous with Cisco Systems (CSCO)—it was, and still is, the worldwide leader in networking equipment. The company also allowed for vendors and suppliers of a company to integrate and better understand their customers' needs and senses of timing.

This monstrous period of technology capital spending spawned some magnificent new companies like Microsoft, Oracle Systems, Dell Computer, Comcast, BEA Systems and SAP Corp.; it also brought on the resurgence of IBM. Companies created in the 80s soared in the 90s, rising to multibillions in sales and many more multibillions of market capitalization. Fortunes were made for both employees and shareholders. Productivity gains were visible and measurable.

Let's look at a few examples. In 1994—only 12 years ago—my firm put out a major research report on enterprise software. My French and British clientele didn't want to wait for the mail to deliver this timely paper, so I offered to fax it to them the day it was made public.

In all, I faxed that 14-page report to 43 people in Europe that day. I remember how impressed I was that I could actually send the documents so quickly—it took me three hours to fax them all! Today, that same report would have been e-mailed to all the clients in about 5 minutes.

Another telltale example: in 1999, I was sitting in the back seat of a London taxi on my way to an appointment, when my cell phone rang. I had rented a London-based cell phone—

although now, of course it's cheaper to actually own a British Telecom cell phone.

It was my chief trader back in Minneapolis, telling me he was in touch with a seller of 250,000 shares of Spiegel Catalogue Company. He knew I had a French account that was possibly looking for some stock, and it didn't trade very fluidly, so having that many shares available was an opportunity.

I immediately phoned the French account from my cell phone, and she agreed to buy the stock. I called the trading desk back in Minneapolis and gave them the order, and it was executed. I generated $25,000 of revenues in 10 minutes from the back of a taxi! That never would have happened even 5 or 6 years earlier; there was just no way. You should have seen the tip I gave the driver!

Cutting Edge, Then and Now

Baby Boomers, think back to the typical business trip of late 1970s or early 80s. You had to drive to the airport, get your boarding pass from the ticket counter, walk to the gate, and then you might call in to the office on a pay phone, using a company telephone credit card. You probably thought that was a major advancement!

After that, there would be a few hours where you'd be unreachable. After arriving at your destination, you could call in again on a pay phone. If you needed to get some important papers fast, you could have them faxed to your hotel.

Back then, there was a lot of unproductive time. Now, of course, you probably read e-mails on your cell phone, and if you have any down time at the airport, you can work on your portable laptop. The opportunity to be productive and available to customers or co-workers is virtually 24/7. (Sometimes that's not so good...we Boomers need to relax a bit!)

Fifteen to twenty years ago, you were pretty cutting edge if you had a cell phone—even though back then, they were cumbersome and antennae that seemed to be about a foot long! They were also quite expensive, so their use was primarily limited to business people and the wealthy.

We middle-of-the-roaders were just getting used to our pagers then, when we thought it was so cool to be "beeped" at a ballgame—though it wasn't so cool when it happened at church!

Nowadays, who doesn't have a cell phone? Has anyone seen a pager recently? They're gone, outdated and passé. Cell phones are absolutely critical to our daily lives. Can you go a whole day without yours? If you can, I tip my hat to you because I know I cannot.

My son and daughter are glued to theirs, texting their friends, making weekend plans and, of course, staying in tune with all the developments within their social circles. Cell phones are their way of life.

Back in the 70s and 80s, how did we exist without them? How did we make it without PCs or the Internet? When was the last time you played a cassette or rented a movie on a VHS tape? Those of us who are a bit older even remember the 8-track players in our cars. Darn tape kept getting snagged!

Computers today are almost as common as cell phones. I was on an airplane ride from London to Minneapolis a few months back. I took a walk around the plane and counted 38 passengers with personal computers, doing work, playing games or watching DVDs. It was amazing—there were 212 total passengers on the plane, and almost 1 in 5 were on their PCs.

I counted 16 individual DVD players as well. So there were 54 passengers enjoying technology that was either nonexistent or prohibitively expensive 15 years ago.

Keeping Up With Advancing Technology

Technology advances in the automobile industry have been stunning as well. These days we don't have to get tune-ups until 60,000 to 100,000 miles, and oil changes are now every 15,000 miles, versus the 3,000-mile rule before.

Every automobile is now a collection of mini-computers with easily learned controls. A mechanic needs more computer and diagnostic training than actual auto training! Whatever happened to the carburetor? I never hear the fateful words, "You need a new head gasket" anymore—and what was a head gasket, anyway?

Auto manufacturers now offer much longer warranties because you'll know in the first week if the car is a lemon or not—the circuitry either works or it doesn't. The mini-computers are either synced-up or they are not. There are actually very few moving parts.

Two of the greatest technological innovations for the automobile in the last 25 years are the anti-lock braking and airbag systems. These two advances are controlled by mini-computers with narrowly defined but critical functions. The semiconductor chip technology advances employed in these two life-saving features have made them relatively inexpensive for manufacturers.

The interior of the car has become more of a cockpit, with a 6-CD changer/player, GPS navigational systems and complex climate controls. The luxury of the DVD player is now virtually standard. Air conditioning—remember when it was the ultimate luxury option? Now, pretty much standard. The technology behind the air-conditioning system costs the auto manufacturer less than $100 to make and install.

The technology and communications systems that we enjoy today, that we take for granted and that make us angry when they're not working, are the result of semiconductor chip technology. The advances of the "chip" fall under Moore's Law.

Gordon Moore was one of the founders of Intel Corporation. In 1965, he stated that computing power would double with each "new generation" of semiconductor chip—or every 18 to 24 months. The speed and the power of the microprocessor would also double with each new cycle. Hence the extreme speed of your $1,000 PC doing computations that 30 years ago took much more time—and back then, the computer itself was the size of a closet.

We are almost at the point where computing power is too much for the average person's needs. The best analogy I've heard was from an Intel engineer who said, "We now have a 300 hp engine running a lawn mower. It really is getting to be too much." More on the semiconductor space later in this chapter.

The PC has come down in price and will continue to do so. A well-loaded PC can be bought for less than $1,000. Dell is advertising the $699 laptop with "Intel Inside," of course.

A Toshiba executive told me his company can probably get to a $300 price point with enough functionality and memory to be competitive. He blushed when I asked him what, if any, profitability there would be for Toshiba's bottom line. I surmised it would be very, very little at those levels.

Intel processors and Microsoft operating systems are not decreasing their prices commensurately. The operating margins for the companies are nearly obscene on those critical systems.

The iPod will change the landscape of the personal communication devices. As I discussed in *Stop Losing Money Today*, the iPod, from Apple Computer, is indeed a phenomenon. Apple has sold roughly 50 million units to about 20 to 25 million unique users. Many of these users have bought second or third units because of increased functionality.

Two dynamics are at work here: one, functionality gets better and more sophisticated, *e.g.*, video capability and holding up to 7,500 songs. Two, the prices will continue to keep coming down, making the iPod affordable for virtually everyone.

Apple is working on two important developments for the iPod: one allowing iTunes to be downloaded wirelessly and the other turning the iPod into a cell phone.

Apple recently sold its 350 millionth song from the iTunes store, clearly having achieved critical mass. With the ability to sell songs from the catalogue on a wireless basis, the company's volume could pick up in a huge way. It's all about "makin' it easy."

When the cell phone capability is available—which will happen, rumor has it, in early 2007—Apple will instantly emerge as a major player in that market. I'll discuss Apple in depth later in the chapter as one of the stocks to own for the future.

As I mentioned earlier, the cellular telephone is a critical component of daily life. Nokia, Samsung, Motorola, Palm, BlackBerry, Sprint, Verizon—the list of manufacturers and providers goes on and on. Costs are now low enough that our children live on these devices, always texting and IMing.

Hundreds of millions of units are sold worldwide and in fact, many users do not have traditional landline phones anymore. The carriers have made the pricing plans affordable for the masses. The cell phone has become a preferred delivery method for e-mails and quick text messages.

The cell phone is blurring borders around the world. We are getting better technology, at low cost, for worldwide texting and clear voice reception. I mentioned earlier that my daughter called me in London from Minneapolis, her cell phone to my Minneapolis-based cell phone number, and the reception was perfectly clear. It does not matter if you are next door or halfway around the world—connectivity is seamless and of high quality.

But where do we go from here? From an investment point of view, it is difficult to make money consistently from the cell phone vendors, component makers and base station manufacturers.

The component makers, like RF Micro Devices (RFMD), Skyworks (SWKS), Powerwave Technologies (PWAV) and Anadigics (ANAD) work on very thin gross margins; therefore, we see razor-thin to nonexistent operating profit margins. These companies can sometimes be decent trades as a new component cycle arrives, but don't blink because the cycle whizzes by quickly and prices begin to drop again. The manufacturers of the cell phones are constantly pressing these companies to drive down component pricing.

The winner in this space is Qualcomm (QCOM), which has filed for over 2,400 patents and has had over 800 patents awarded. It is the leader and pioneer in code division multiplication access (CDMA), the technology driver for third-generation (3G) phones. Europe and Asia began their migration to 3G in late 2003, and the United States began the 3G move in mid-2005—and it continues.

Qualcomm has enviable operating profit margins in the mid-40 percents and they are sustainable. The company licenses its technology to more than 50 cell phone manufacturers, thus the very high and sustainable margins. With patent protection and the patent portfolio growing, Qualcomm is not pressed on pricing and can maintain its margins.

Riding the Broadband Wave

Broadband connectivity is the biggest goal of carriers and networking companies like Cisco Systems (CSCO) and Juniper Networks (JNPR). The more information you can drive down the "pipe," and the faster you can make it go, the more applications and consumer goodies can be delivered and charged for.

The drive for broadband is both wireless and landline. We all remember hooking up our modems and using our telephone lines to access the Internet. The connectivity was slow and tedious—forget about opening or downloading large files. It took forever.

We Baby Boomers now get frustrated if an airport or hotel doesn't have broadband or wireless access.

All this has developed in the last 10 years, but more intensely in the last 5. All Starbucks stores offer wireless access, which has become a great marketing tool for the company. "Wifi" has become another new word in our vocabulary!

Broadband availability has been very important in building consumer-friendly businesses. Yahoo!, Google, AOL, MSN and other search engines and major portals began seeing real scale in their business models as broadband became more prevalent.

Online retailers and services have become major businesses with the broadband growth. How many of you Boomers begin your travel plans by checking online travel sites like Expedia, Orbitz and Priceline? How many of you check out Amazon's review of a book before buying it?

If we still had slow, dial-up connectivity, would we surf so many Internet sites, or would we just go to the one that we had to for business or critical consumer needs?

Broadband access is also spawning new security measures for these connections. We expect that our transactions and exchanges of personal information remain secured and encrypted. VeriSign (VRSN) is the leader in Website digital certificates; that is, the company secures the connection between the consumer and the vendor's server that handles the transaction. Its encrypted connections have never been hacked into or intercepted.

With the proliferation of wireless, security is not as guaranteed, so we will see newer companies emerge with security and encryption solutions for wireless communiqués and transactions. Again, VeriSign will be a leader there, but not the only player.

Internet Security Systems (ISSX) and SonicWALL (SNWL) are two other public players. There are several privately held companies that are making inroads, and those that gain critical mass or superiority of product will make it to the public markets or be acquired by larger companies.

The world of software is going through changes that could significantly alter their entrenched financial models. The software giants from the 1980s and 90s are presently at risk. The operating margins in software are typically quite lucrative, ranging from the low teen percents to the mid-40 percents. It is very difficult to kill software companies quickly; they tend to linger for a long time because of the high margins.

Examples of the giants of the 80s, 90s and early 2000s, companies that helped modernize enterprises, are Microsoft (MSFT), Oracle Systems (ORCL), PeopleSoft (acquired by Oracle in late 2004), BEA Systems (BEAS), SAP Corp. (SAP), Siebel Systems (also acquired by Oracle in 2005), Borland (BORL), Novell (NOVL), Adobe (ADBE) and Autodesk (ADSK), among many others.

Once a software system has been installed into an enterprise, it is difficult to remove it or replace it. No company wants to "shut down" a mission critical application to try a new competitor's product, and no chief information officer is going to admit that he or she was wrong and that there may be a better mousetrap out there.

So, the entrenched vendor collects maintenance and upgrade fees year in and year out. That's why so many mediocre software companies have managed to hang on.

With the technology capital spending previously mentioned, many corporations did vastly increase their productivity and actually manage their costs better by buying and installing enterprise-wide software programs. Oracle Systems owns the database market; Microsoft owns the "office suite" with their Office software; BEA Systems owns the application server market; PeopleSoft owns the human resource applications; and Siebel Systems owns the customer relationship market. (Again, both PeopleSoft and Siebel are now part of Oracle Systems.)

These stocks, however, are stuck in the mud and not providing good returns for their shareholders in spite of their great profitability and enviable operating margins.

Why? The law of large numbers is working against these companies. When a company does $10 billion in annual revenues, growing 10 percent means adding another billion in revenues. That's not an easy task.

Remember, the stock market rewards growth, growth and growth! For example, Oracle Systems finished its 2006 fiscal year on May 31, reporting total revenues of $11.8 billion and operating profits of $4.03 billion, a staggering 34 percent operating margin. The market cap is $80 billion, but as of this writing, the stock has had a narrow trading range the past 52 weeks of $11.75 to $15.21.

Oracle is the leading database company in the world by far, and now with recent acquisitions, it's a strong applications player. But the stock isn't going to go up until the company can demonstrate consistent top-line revenue growth and, with that, earnings growth. The market doesn't reward stagnation.

Software and Semiconductors

What's happening in the software world? What's changing and who is the leading horse, the one to watch?

To start with, Salesforce.com (CRM) is changing the software model. This is the company to own for the next five to seven years. It offers a "Customer Relationship Manager" program— hence the symbol CRM.

Salesforce.com has pioneered the "hosted model," which means that there is nothing to install on the customer's end. Salesforce.com hosts the application and sells it on an as-needed basis. Customers can scale the product in at their own pace instead of tying up their own database assets, making the cost is significantly less than a multimillion-dollar installation from Siebel Systems.

With these advantages, Salesforce.com has generated a consistent 90-plus percent customer satisfaction rating in independent surveys, which is a stunning number for a software company. Typically, software companies are thrilled if satisfaction surveys come in around 55 to 60 percent. With Salesforce.com's significantly higher average, add-on sales from existing companies are almost guaranteed.

"The world does not go 'round without semiconductors." This was told to me by a senior engineer at Intel Corp (INTC), and he was right. There is no new electronic product, no new PC, no new iPod, no new automobile function, without a semiconductor chip leading the way and defining the functionality.

The world of semiconductors is huge and geographically diverse, with many different players, large and small. Great semiconductor technology has brought down the prices of some cool consumer products like the DVD player, the iPod, the personal computer, the HDTV set and the digital camera, to name a few.

The leading company in the space is Intel Corp., with a market capitalization of $105 billion as of this writing and operating margins in the 30 to 32 percent range. The company did $38 billion of revenues in calendar year 2005, earned $12 billion in pre-tax profits and paid more than $4 billion in federal income taxes—and yet the stock has been a dog for the past year or so. Why? Simple answer: no real top-line growth.

The semiconductor stocks are great to trade but not to own long term. The cycles come and go, and pricing pressure abounds from the Taiwanese, Chinese and Korean competitors. A semiconductor company can make a great new chip for a DVD player or an HDTV set, but the technology advantage may last only three to six months.

It is difficult to build a financial model for any period longer than one year. The earnings and revenue expectations can go up and down like a yo-yo.

Because the group tends to go up and down together, there is very little stock price independence in this sector. Intel has been going down in 2006, about 40 percent off its 52-week high, and so has its main competitor, Advanced Micro Devices (AMD).

Other big names in semi-land have had a difficult 2006, like Xilinx (XLNX), SanDisk (SNDK) and Marvell Technology (MRVL). All these companies are off significantly from their 52-week high. These are well-managed companies that will stand the test of time, but no matter how terrific they look, as far as their stocks go, it will be better to trade than invest for a two to four-year period.

Once the group begins to head up, it is a great sign for the general technology market because semiconductors are the first component necessary for new electronic and computing products. Semiconductor companies are the bellwether for the IBMs, the Dells and the Hewlett-Packards.

The opposite action is also true. As semiconductor companies begin to slow, all the other major technology companies will follow one or two quarters later. Again, remember—these stocks tend to be dates, not marriages!

Product Tracking in This Day and Age

One sector of technology that falls into the "where do we go from here" category is radio frequency identification (RFID). This is a method of automatic identification that relies on radio waves to store and remotely retrieve data by using RFID tags or transponders that can be incorporated into a product (or even an animal or a person). You haven't heard much about this technology because there are very few public company players in the sector.

First, a quick bit of history. At the grocery store, the cashier runs your purchases over a scanner that reads barcodes, identifying the items and their prices. Simple enough: the barcode is synced up with the cash register, you receive an itemized tally, you pay your bill and off you go.

But think back for a moment. The barcode technology was patented in 1952 but didn't really become important until 30 years later, when they began to hit the general retail market in 1982. At that time, 15,000 suppliers slapped them on their products. By 1987, that number jumped up to 75,000—a huge increase, fivefold in five years.

What caused that massive increase? Wal-Mart. That was the first retailer to demand that all its suppliers be barcode-compliant, and if you wanted to sell to Wal-Mart, you were just that—end of argument.

Well, here and now, Wal-Mart is at it again. Now it wanted all its main suppliers to be RFID-compliant by 2005, which was last year. Extensions were granted, though, because some were slow to implement, but they're getting on track. In the next five to six years, all Wal-Mart suppliers will be RFID-ready or they won't be Wal-Mart suppliers anymore. So, just as Wal-Mart drove the barcode industry, it will drive the RFID industry.

The Department of Defense is the other driver of this technology. Currently, all 270,000 military cargo containers are RFID-tagged and traceable through 40 countries around the world.

RFID tags have been available for the last five years, but the technology is becoming more sophisticated. The tag itself, the tag reader and the middleware software that tracks and traces the item's whereabouts are all necessary. The technology is far more sophisticated than the simple barcode, which is read-only and once scanned, is rendered useless. The RFID tag can take on that same road map, but it can also stay alive for as long as it is programmed for.

For example, Michelin Tire is placing RFID tags in all its new tires—roughly a million a year—so that it can pinpoint the exact location of any tire it has sold anywhere in the world.

Another example: A major casino has placed RFID tags on 80,000 uniforms to track employees' whereabouts, to help prevent theft.

Another: Gillette has ordered 500 million RFID tags to track and inventory its pallets of deodorant, shaving cream and razors.

The cost per chip is currently about $0.50, which may seem prohibitively expensive to simply track an individual can of shaving cream. But as the cost per RFID tag is predicted to fall to about $0.05 apiece, then the individual, small consumer item can be tagged and monitored.

Other practical uses for the RFID tags are for vital

documents such as passports, driver's licenses, university diplomas, birth certificates and company ID badges.

Ethicists and politicians will debate the invasion of privacy issues on this one for years to come. One ethical question: should a manufacturer of simple consumer products "RFID" the actual products, or just the packaging?

Gillette should care about its shaving products' movement in the marketplace and their ability to manage inventory and understand geographical preferences. But do you also want Gillette to know how often and at what time you shave or use its deodorant?

I understand Delta Airlines (DAL) temporarily puts RFID tags on all checked luggage to prevent lost bags and all the annoyances that go with that fun exercise, but the tags will be disabled once the bag is claimed. Now that works!

RFID will become a major technology megatrend in the very near future, no question about it. There are many private companies that are developing the technology with cheaper tags and cheaper readers.

There are two public companies that play in the space, and we Boomers must be aware of them because they could become very relevant stocks.

The first one is Manhattan Associates, Inc. (MANH), the software company that can provide the vital middleware programs needed to implement an RFID system for any manufacturer. Currently, RFID is a small piece of MANH's business, as their principal endeavor is supply chain software.

MANH's market capitalization is about $605 million. It does about $250 million per year in revenues and has operating profit margins in the 15 to 18 percent range.

The other player, the one that has the biggest opportunity

to dominate the RFID space, is VeriSign Corp. (VRSN), a $4.1 billion market capitalization company that is the keeper of all dot-com and dot-net Internet addresses. All dot-com and dot-net e-mails and Website lookups go through VeriSign's data center, over 10 billion times per day.

VRSN also handles about 10 million cell phone connections per day with its secure sockets layer (SSL) network, for security in transmissions. The company is the leader in Website digital certificates, which allows us consumers to put our financial and other sensitive information online because it encrypts the data connection. As mentioned earlier, it has never been hacked or intercepted.

VeriSign is the true utility and traffic cop of the Internet. Its database has the capacity to assign an Internet protocol (IP) address to every RFID tag, thus positioning the company as the backbone of the RFID world. VeriSign could assign billions of RFID-tagged IP addresses *daily*. Because of it's security strength and IP address capability, most major companies will allow their RFID work to be handled by VRSN.

The company has an incredible opportunity to own the space, but it has been very, very low key about this technology. It has quietly been consulting and helping many corporations to understand the RFID world, but again, it has been done without much fanfare.

Major revenues won't really begin until 2008 or 2009, but the growth could be exponential; coupled with its other dominant businesses, VeriSign could grow to be a $50 billion market capitalization company. Currently, it does about $1.8 billion to $1.9 billion of revenues, with operating profit margins above 20 percent.

The following are some interesting technology companies

with a brief discussion of their core fundamentals. These companies could prove to be the leaders in this decade, and hopefully the next.

Potential Booming Technology Stocks for Baby Boomers

Apple Computer (AAPL)

Apple has two main product categories: the Macintosh computer system, with its software add-ons, and the popular iPod, an MP3 device.

Apple has sold more than 50 million iPod units to over 20 million consumers. Upgrade cycles and add-on services such as video are available, attracting new buyers and causing existing customers to buy again. In the future, the iPod will have new functionality including wireless downloads of iTunes music and cell phone functionality.

Apple's market share of the MP3 market is roughly 70 percent. The new Mac computer is also making inroads into Apple's core customer base (pardon the pun), which consists of consumers, the educational market and the artistic/engineering market. The new Mac could begin to grab market share from Dell and Compaq.

Apple has brilliantly opened several retail stores, 150 in total, which allow the company to control its customers' major purchases as well as handle the peripherals sales.

Apple's current market cap of $54 billion is about 2.5 times 2006 revenues and about 2 times the 2007 revenue forecast. Apple's earnings are accelerating very quickly, from $1.44 in 2005 to an estimate of $2.70 in 2007—a near double. Stock should be bought and owned for the next 3 to 5 years.

aQuantive, Inc. (AQNT)

The leader in the growing Internet advertising/marketing industry, aQuantive has three main divisions: digital marketing technologies, digital performance media and digital marketing services.

AQNT designs complex Websites and then monitors performance with proprietary technology. The megatrend is that traditional advertising spending is migrating more and more to the Internet, and AQNT is the go-to company.

Management is conservative in its revenue and earnings guidance, thus not letting analysts get ahead of themselves. This company could be an $8 billion to $10 billion market capitalization company in the next 3 to 6 years. It's got a great story and great execution by the management team.

Procter & Gamble, one of aQuantive's clients, is leading the way in moving advertising and marketing spending from traditional outlets to the Internet.

Autodesk, Inc. (ADSK)

Autodesk has been around since 1982. This company dominates the two-dimensional computer-aided design (CAD) space with over 6 million customers.

As ADSK migrates to three-dimensional designs, customer follow-on sales should be fairly smooth. ADSK is the biggest vendor in the architectural, infrastructure and civil design, and manufacturing industries. It has also become a major player in the media software space.

Earnings have been very consistent with no real surprises. Management has been superb and communicates very well with Wall Street. Stock has been off due to real estate slowdown, but the architectural division is only about 10 percent of ADSK revenue base.

ADSK has a reseller base of over 2,000 vendors, allowing for solid worldwide distribution. It's a solid story for the next 3-plus years.

CheckFree Corp. (CKFR)

CKFR is the leading provider of financial electronic commerce service and makes proprietary software for electronic commerce as well. Currently, 14 million consumers receive and pay bills over the Internet or through their financial services provider.

CKFR's biggest customer is the Bank of America, delivering roughly 18 percent of the company's revenues. Bank of America has been very aggressive in marketing bill-payment services to its own customers.

Other customers for CKFR include Wachovia Bank and Wells Fargo Bank. The strong trend is to drive consumers to this bill-review and payment methodology. CKFR has minimal competition in the space and will continue to dominate.

CKFR has maintained strong operating margins in the high 20 percents and could rise to 30 to 32 percent. It has solid management, and the CEO is also the founder.

Opsware, Inc. (OPSW)

This sub-$1 billion market capitalization story has the opportunity to be one of the great software stories of this decade and the next. Opsware could be the Oracle/BEA Systems/Siebel Systems/PeopleSoft of the future. As these companies dominated their respective spaces in the 1990s and early 2000s, OPSW could do the same for the next 10 years.

OPSW's software automates server and software operations in large data centers. Provisioning and updating a large server farm—meaning 10,000 servers or more—normally takes days because traditionally it's done manually, and it's a very expensive and time-intensive process. OPSW software can do the same functions in hours, thus saving large enterprises millions of dollars of cost.

OPSW has seeded its market with huge customers such as EDS, FedEx, the British government and Cisco Systems. In fact, CSCO will resell OPSW product to its own customer base beginning in mid-2006, with real meaningful sales occurring in 2007.

OPSW has recently launched a mid-market product to attract smaller customers and is allowing larger customers to phase in its software. It also recently purchased a private company called Rendition Networks that will serve the networking equipment.

Huge networks installed by Cisco, Extreme Networks, Lucent and many others can now be provisioned and updated in an automated process. This product line has doubled the size of OPSW's addressable market.

OPSW could be a 10-bagger over the next 4 to 6 years. The founder is technology guru Marc Andreessen, co-founder of Netscape and credited with inventing the Internet browser while a student at the University of Illinois.

Progressive Gaming International Corp. (PGIC)

PGIC is a turnaround story and has had a few fumbles along the way, but the opportunity in front of this company is staggering.

It used to be a hardware company to the gaming industry that carried horrible margins and unpredictable sales cycles. Under new management, this company is transforming itself to a software model and retiring debt left over from old management.

In essence, Progressive Gaming International has a server-based slot machine product that allows casinos to place "dumb terminals," costing about $1,000 each, in place of expensive slot machines that cost $10,000 to $12,000 each and require expensive maintenance.

Dumb terminals require minimal servicing and are programmed from a central server that allows the casino operator to change the theme of the slot machine on the fly. PGIC will collect a $1 per day royalty per machine—all high margins.

Also, PGIC has developed the patented Intelligent Table system, which is a radio frequency identification device (RFID)-based product for the Blackjack game. With this system, customers use chips that fitted with RFID tags, allowing the casino to monitor who is playing, when they are playing and how much they are playing for.

The table retrofit cost is about $4,500 per, plus the cost of the RFID chips. PGIC will sell the tables and the chips, and command a per-day fee of $6 per table—an enviable model, with high margins.

The barriers to entry are quite high, as each casino vendor must be approved by the various state commissions, but PGIC has all its necessary approvals.

The other major opportunity is international, where PGIC has excellent relationships and distribution. Casino and gaming growth is stronger internationally than in the United States.

This company has begun the turnaround process and should see strong revenues and earnings trends beginning in the third quarter of 2006 and beyond. I believe PGIC will eventually be acquired by a larger operator/vendor like IGT Corp., but the run in the meantime could be fun to watch and invest in.

Qualcomm, Inc. (QCOM)
Qualcomm is the world's leader in wireless code division multiplication access (CDMA) and mobile communications.

The company has more than 2,400 patents filed, with over 800 having been granted. The company licenses its technology to more than 50 cell phone handset manufacturers and infrastructure vendors.

QCOM sports operating margins currently at 45 percent and they could rise to 48 to 49 percent as third generation (3G) handsets become more available in the marketplace. This story is already a monster, with a $55 billion market capitalization, but Qualcomm could double that valuation over the next 3 to 4 years.

Salesforce.com (CRM)

Salesforce.com is a pioneer in the hosted model for software application. Its Customer Relationship Manager program is making in-roads against its main competitor, Siebel Systems, a division of Oracle Systems.

CRM's system is an on-demand product, and customers basically have a monthly subscription arrangement. Customer flexibility to add or delete "seats" is also on a monthly basis. Installation is nonexistent, as Salesforce.com hosts the application for the customer, thus not tying up the customer's database assets. New user training normally takes just a few hours, and the support team at CRM is 24/7.

Salesforce.com was initially successful in seeding the market with small to medium-sized enterprises but has made some serious penetration into larger accounts. Two reference accounts are Merrill Lynch, Inc. and Cisco Systems, Inc.

Salesforce.com has minimal earnings currently, as it has spent an enormous amount in sales and marketing—roughly 50 to 55 percent of its revenues. This expense will come down over the next 2 to 3 years, driving operating margins to a comfortable and normalized 25 to 30 percent.

CRM will produce other applications that it will sell into

its base, such as human resource and financial systems. Salesforce.com is a paradigm shift in the way software will be sold and managed. It's a tremendous, long-term story.

Symantec, Inc. (SYMC)

Symantec provides solutions to both the enterprise sector and the individual consumer to secure their information technology systems. Its best-known product is the Norton AntiVirus protection system, which works on both Windows and Mac computers.

About 14 months ago, Symantec bought a similarly sized company, Veritas Software, which was very relevant in the server and storage management business. Since then it's been going through the pains of a large merger. With that stage is behind it, though, we could see it restart growth in calendar 2007. It might be a quarter or two early, but the downside here is minimal.

Symantec has a market capitalization of $17.5 billion, with expected 2007 revenues around $5.3 billion. It has operating profit margins in the 30 to 32 percent range—very enviable. If it resumes decent revenue growth over the next year or so, Symantec could double in price.

ValueClick, Inc. (VCLK)

ValueClick is a worldwide marketing services company that allows its customers to advertise and market their products through various online channels. It offers customized solutions for search engine marketing and e-mail and lead-generation campaigns.

Its technology division sells infrastructure tools that allow its users to customize and manage their online display and marketing campaigns. ValueClick is a major player in this growing and emerging online space.

VCLK could be a great acquisition candidate because a larger media concern should want to grow in this burgeoning industry. In the meantime, with nearly $300 million in cash and a 30 percent earnings growth rate, VLCK stock should be a stalwart performer.

VeriSign, Inc. (VRSN)

VeriSign is the true utility and traffic cop of the Internet. All dot-com and dot-net addresses are managed by VRSN and all dot-com and dot-net transmissions go through the VRSN database.

The company is also a leader in payment systems, security on the Web—with the Website digital certificate program—and the transmitter of millions of cell phone connections through its SSL systems. VRSN has a content division that distributes cell phone ring tones through various national and international telecom carriers and a nascent RFID division that could prove to be the next leg of major growth for the next 10 years.

VRSN has a market capitalization of $4.1 billion and revenues are approaching $2.0 billion, with high cash flow and solid earnings. It could become a very big, large-cap company. VRSN was admitted to the S&P 500 in early 2006.

VitalStream Holdings, Inc. (VSTH)

VitalStream is a major player in the emerging content delivery network (CDN) space. Its technology allows its customers to produce streaming video for the Internet. This company plays in the business-to-business sector because its tool set will allow users to customize both audio and video streaming, mostly for advertising purposes.

VSTH will do about $26 million of revenues in 2006 and

earnings will break even. However, 2007 will be exciting, as it could do $40 million of revenues and earn $0.25 per share.

This is a newer technology space dominated by Akamai, Inc. (AKAM), but VSTH is making terrific inroads. It will likely acquire small niche technology companies to help round out its product offerings.

As I previously mentioned, the semiconductor space has been in a general downturn in 2006. As the sector begins to stabilize, there will be some very attractive stocks to buy such as Intel, Advanced Micro Devices, Marvell and many others. But, that time has not yet arrived—at least not as of this writing!

For more technology stock ideas and further discussion, including current prices, initial price targets, market capitalization, addressable market size, competitive landscape, earnings per share forecasts, growth rates and PE and PEG ratio analysis, please refer to my website, www.investingbabyboomer.com.

CHAPTER SIX

ALTERNATIVE ENERGY:
JUST FOLLOW THE MONEY

WHENEVER I HEAR ABOUT A POSSIBLE POLITICAL SCANDAL BREWING, I think back to the line from the movie *All the President's Men:* "Just follow the money." The money trail tends to lead one right to the center of the scandal.

Well, that same sentiment can now be said for the alternative energy industry, where the venture capital backing has been going higher and is continuing to do so—but more on that later.

Introducing Alternative Energy

We Baby Boomers remember when a gallon of gasoline was less than a dollar and a typical fill-up may have been $15 to $18. We didn't like it, but we were always reminded that gasoline was 4 to 5 times more expensive in Europe.

In our youth, we loved powerful cars with suped-up engines, but of course, we steadily migrated to family-type and sports utility vehicles (SUVs) in our "responsible" years. Now, many of us Boomers are yearning for comfortable luxury cars because we've "earned" them, or for nice sports cars so we can return to our carefree youths.

But throughout this entire cycle, we never really overpaid for gasoline. We saw it jump in price during the oil crisis of 1973 and 1979, but it settled back down. We only remember the long lines at the local gas stations when supply was temporarily in jeopardy.

The "crisis" was dealt with, and we all went about our business. We talked about our reliance on foreign oil, and OPEC became a four-letter word. We were inconvenienced, but not to the point where a groundswell of change was in order.

I have hosted British and French professional portfolio managers in the San Francisco-San Jose-Silicon Valley area over the past 16 years on 55 different occasions, visiting up to 20 companies in 5 days. Typically, we would drive about 400 to 500 miles in a week during these visits.

Every time I pulled into a gas station, the British and French managers would marvel at the low cost to fill up the SUV I had rented. In Europe, an SUV was a true luxury not because of the vehicle's price, but because of the cost to keep the tank full!

During the last 25 years, many of us paid lip service to the need for alternative energy. It sounded great, but we figured, let some alfalfa-head figure it out because filling up our tanks was not that expensive or painful. Solar energy was a neat idea, but we decided to leave it up to the 70s hippies—let them put it in their own homes.

After all, heating my home wasn't that expensive, and besides, I had that fancy, puffy stuff—ah, insulation—put into my new addition. Plus, I put in those energy-efficient windows that promised to keep heating and air-conditioning bills low. I did my part to help with energy conservation, and I didn't even have a ponytail!

Well, now we are facing gasoline prices over $3 a gallon

and our home heating bills have more than doubled. This trend is now a reality. There will be no going back to $1 a gallon or having our heating bills cut in half. We are adding new words to our vocabulary again such as *hybrid auto, ethanol-based fuel, fuel cells*, and *wind power*. As of this writing, the price of oil is touching $75 per barrel. We have instability in the Middle East, Iran is saber rattling and due to infrastructural insufficiencies, Iraq is not yet producing supply. In fact, it will need a few years to rebuild its production systems.

To compound this problem, demand is now significantly and rapidly increasing in India and China as they industrialize. China is now the second largest importer of oil in the world, and it is consuming more than 35 percent of the increase in oil consumption. This is not going to lessen, and China will only require more energy resources as it continues to build out its infrastructure and develop its new world economy.

If you are a shareholder of Exxon Mobil Corporation, you are the partial owner of a company whose market capitalization is $411 billion—the most valuable company in the world. It is also sitting on $32 billion in cash as of March 31, 2006.

If you own Exxon Mobil shares, you are the partial owner of a company that did $377 billion of revenues the last 12 months (June, September and December 2005, and March 31 quarter, 2006) and that reported after-tax profits of nearly $37 billion the last four quarters (again, that's four quarters ending March 31, 2006). That's $37 billion of after-tax profit! It also paid $25 billion in federal income taxes for those four quarters.

If you have held this stock for the last three years, your share value has doubled—not to mention that the dividend increased during that time as well. With all of these numbers flying around, do you want oil prices to fall? Probably not.

However, since most of us don't own oil stock and energy is now absorbing more of what's in our wallets and in the checkbooks of businesses and industries, we are beginning to seriously address the issue. President Bush said it well in his 2006 State of the Union address: "We are addicted to oil." Now is the time to search for and develop alternatives.

Here Comes the Sun...

The Germans and the Japanese are far ahead of the rest of the world when it comes to solar energy. The two countries represent 70 percent of the solar wafers and panels sold through 2005, and both governments have given their consumer and business communities incentives to go the solar route.

In fact, 6 of the top 10 manufacturers of solar panels and peripherals are either Japanese or German; the other four originate in other European countries. The Sharp Corporation of Japan is the single largest, with a 25 percent market share.

The United States represents about 10 percent of the world's solar installations. Currently, California is leading the way, giving local incentives and rebates for solar installations.

In early 2006, the California Public Utilities Commission passed a solar initiative for an 11-year, $3.2 billion program, with plans to install 3,000 MW of new solar-generation power. This initiative is aimed primarily at the residential market.

The principal problem right now is the limited supply of silicon, which provides the photovoltaic effect and converts solar rays into electricity. As the supply goes up and down, this will cause volatility in the various solar energy stocks. Expectations are for supply to even out in mid-2007.

There are only a few publicly traded companies in the solar space that have any kind of critical mass or decent profitability: Evergreen Solar (ESLR), Suntech Power (STP) and SunPower (SPWR). These three combined have a market capitalization of $6.3 billion and combined, their revenue expectations for calendar year 2007 is about $1.2 billion.

Suntech Power is the largest and is headquartered in China, which does not give professional portfolio managers any comfort. There are a lot of little players, mostly private, working on some hybrid type technologies for solar, but nothing that is publicly investible yet.

Pumping Money Into the New Fuel

Remember I said to follow the money? If you go back to 1990, the Internet was in its infancy. In fact, AOL was formally introduced in 1991, went public in 1992 and announced it had amassed 500,000 subscribers in December 1993.

Back then, the Internet was "a thing on the come." Yahoo! was not founded until 1995, a short 11 years ago! And Google was founded in January 1996 as a research project.

What gave the Internet the great surge in the early 1990s was venture capital funding and sponsorship. The geniuses who founded the Internet service companies, retail concepts, portals and search firms received a wave of venture funding that allowed for proper development of their concepts.

The venture capitalists were patient, as they collectively understood the Internet to be massive in scale and worldwide in scope. The money flowed to the entrepreneurs and many developed companies that sustain to this day—but some developed flops that shall remain on the ash heap and will always be great answers in a game of Trivial Pursuit. Remember DrKoop.com? Shopnow.com? Vitamins.com?

This same phenomenon is now occurring in the alternative energy space. Venture capital funding is happening at a very aggressive pace. Cleantech Venture Network, LLC, a research firm headquartered in Ann Arbor, Michigan, states that alternative energy investments will claim about 7 percent of overall venture capital funding in 2006, versus 2 percent back in 2001.

Since 1999, about $7.5 billion has been invested in these alternative technologies, and it is predicted that another $8.5 billion will follow from 2006 through 2009.

This does not include the projects being funded by Chevron Corp. (CVX), Exxon Mobil Corp. (XOM) and General Electric Corp. (GE). Exxon Mobil and Chevron have seen their revenues explode over the last three years and being smart companies, their research and development budgets have also kept pace. They are somewhat quiet and secretive about their research, but alternative energy projects are certainly part of their agenda.

Many of the venture capital funding projects have to do with making solar energy more cost-efficient and less reliant on silicon. Also, ethanol will be important as we move along because it is an efficient fuel with minimal emissions and its main resource is boundless: largely, it's made out of corn.

Brazil serves as the model for these projects because it is totally energy independent, with ethanol being its principal fuel for autos. The U.S. has E10, a 90 percent gasoline/10 percent ethanol mixture. All autos sold in the United States are E10-compliant.

E85 is 15 percent unleaded gasoline and 85 percent ethanol. There are about 4 million FFVs—flexible fuel vehicles—in the United States and more are on the way from the auto manufacturers. Gasoline stations are refitting their pumps to accommodate the E85 mixture. So, help is on the way!

From an investment point of view, the alternative energy space is a difficult one to play. Research on these companies is not yet mainstream, and the ability to have large stock positions for mutual funds is also somewhat limiting.

Mutual funds will own Toyota Motors (TM) as the hybrid auto play. Toyota leads the auto industry in successfully marketing its hybrid autos, which feature half-electric and half-combustible engines.

The models called the Prius Hybrid, the Camry Hybrid and the Highlander Hybrid SUV all carry decent sticker prices and dealers have no incentive to discount them, as demand is quite high. The miles per gallon are very impressive, ranging from 58, highway and city in the Prius to 30 for the Highlander.

The money saved in fuel costs—assuming $3 per gallon and driving 75 miles per day—range from $2,600 with the Prius to $1,300 with the Highlander. These numbers are impressive, but Toyota prices the Hybrid line well enough above the comparable model that the economics are not quite there yet.

As the hybrid models from other auto manufacturers begin to hit the market, pricing will become more in line and make the economics more sensible.

The important thing for Baby Boomer investors to keep in mind is that hybrid technology is available and will become mainstream in our auto-buying habits. The alternative energy space must be kept on the Boomers' radar screen, as we have seen funding in the space explode and what normally follows something like that is a series of discoveries and initial public offerings.

That formula sounds simple but hearkens back to the Internet space in the early 1990s. Many of the IPOs were suspect companies with profit-proof business models, and eventually they did end up on the ash heap.

But there were some monstrous successes and fortunes generated for the shareholders and the original venture capital backers. Many of those companies changed and enhanced our lives, and I believe the same will occur with the alternative energy sector.

We will see some goofy companies try to go public and we will see some that are great and life-changing as well. The important fact to consider is who is or can be profitable versus who has a neat science or concept but cannot really monetize it profitably.

But it is critical that we Boomers keep our investment eyes—not to mention our civic eyes—on these future players.

Potential Booming Alternative Energy Stocks for Baby Boomers

The Andersons, Inc. (ANDE)

The Andersons company is headquartered in southern Ohio and has grain elevator facilities in Ohio, Indiana, Illinois and Michigan. ANDE refurbishes and resells or re-leases rail cars. The majority of its businesses are fairly low-margin.

However, the new play for ANDE is its joint venture with Marathon Oil (MRO) to build an ethanol plant in Ohio that could produce 110 million gallons of the stuff per year. It has applied for the permit, which is expected to be approved.

The plant could be operational and productive by the first quarter of 2008. This venture could yield greater margins for ANDE and professional portfolio managers could assign a higher-valuation PE, due to the ethanol play.

ANDE is almost the total package: it can store the grain, process it into ethanol and transport it with its own railcar system. The company has a market capitalization of $525 million and a revenue run rate of $1.35 billion. Stock has had a good 2006 but frankly, it is not yet fully discovered.

Archer Daniels Midland, Inc. (ADM)

Archer Daniels Midland is in the business of transporting, storing, processing and merchandising many different agricultural products. As ADM is highly involved with many different grains and seeds, the obvious alternative energy connection is its ability to handle corn, which is vital in the ethanol-making process.

ADM can mill,and process corn, and of course transport the end product. It could be the general play as it has the ability to process other grains as well, and it could emerge as the leader in the whole biofuels industry.

The company has a market capitalization of $27 billion and does revenues in the mid-$30 billions. ADM will be an important player to watch as the ethanol potential unfolds in the United States.

Color Kinetics, Inc. (CLRK)

Color Kinetics provides intelligent solid-state lighting systems (ISSL) using light-emitting diodes (LED). Its systems are available for commercial installations and are arriving into the consumer market.

The alternative energy play here is the massive amount of energy saved by using LED lights—in the 50-plus percent range. The beauty of CLRK is that it owns 50 patents and is applying for approximately 150 more.

The intellectual property that this company has will force many others to form licensing agreements with it. It could also be acquired by General Electric (GE) or Sylvania. Both would love to have such a patent portfolio in their fold.

CLRK is a $300 million market capitalization company with revenue expectations in 2006 and 2007 of $64 million and $83 million respectively, and earnings doubling from $0.22 to $0.46 by 2007.

Harris and Harris Group, Inc. (TINY)

Harris and Harris Group is a public venture capital portfolio of private companies. TINY specializes in the nanotechnology world, with about 15 investments in its portfolio.

Nanotechnology will have commercial implications in the medical device and general materials industries. It also has its place in alternative energy, with potential in the surfaces that are on wind turbines and products in the solar energy line.

TINY is a barometer for what is coming in the nano world. The goal is to mature the portfolio investments and either go public via the IPO route or to merge the private companies with larger corporations.

SunPower Corp. (SPWR)

SunPower manufactures high-purity silicon solar cells, solar panels and inverters. It claims to have the highest yield of any manufacturer, and the National Renewable Energy Laboratory agrees with this assessment.

SPWR focuses on both commercial and residential opportunities, especially where local or national government has tax incentives. The company has been very successful in both Germany and Japan.

The company recently did a secondary stock offering, raising $280 million of fresh capital to go with the $100 million already on the balance sheet. 2006 and 2007 revenues and earnings could grow more than 100 percent. This could be a big story in the ever-growing solar field.

SPWR has contracted for more silicon than was initially planned by analysts. Great upside to this stock.

Suntech Power Holdings Co., Ltd. (STP)

Suntech Power is a major manufacturer and distributor of silicon solar cells and solar panels. It is one of the biggest in the world and is experiencing a huge growth rate in both revenues and earnings.

Revenues for 2006 through 2008 are forecast to grow from $500 million to $1.25 billion, and earnings should go from a 2006 estimate of $0.70 to $1.84 in 2008. The only negative is that professional portfolio managers tend to give this company a discount valuation because Suntech is headquartered in China.

The market capitalization is $4.1 billion. As Suntech progresses through the next four to five quarters, if it is consistent in achieving analysts' estimates, the valuation may expand as credibility is solidified. Right now, this is the biggest public player in the solar panel and cells industry.

Zoltek Companies, Inc. (ZOLT)

Zoltek has been in business since 1975 and it is one of the largest manufacturers of quality, commercial-grade carbon fiber.

Carbon fiber is utilized in several industries including sporting goods, automobiles, oil and gas equipment, and wind turbines. As we search for alternative sources of power in the world, wind turbine generation is becoming more critical. The carbon fiber enables the turbines to be lighter and stronger, thus requiring less maintenance.

ZOLT's market capitalization is $405 million and its revenue base is exploding, nearly tripling between 2005 and 2007. Carbon fiber is in huge demand and ZOLT is committed for all of its production capacity through next year. This could be a huge story for the next 4 to 5 years. ZOLT will probably have to raise equity capital to build out more capacity—a nice problem to have.

For further discussion about earnings and revenue expectations, valuation analysis, competitive landscape, addressable marketplace and overall commentary, please come to my website: www.investingbabyboomer.com.

CHAPTER SEVEN

WHERE DO WE GO FROM HERE?

I HOPE THESE SIX CHAPTERS HAVE ASSISTED YOU with your investment thinking and strategy. In my nearly 28 years of involvement in the investing world, whether advising individual investors, professional portfolio managers or emerging growth companies, the one consistency I have tried to maintain is optimism.

As I write this book in the summer of 2006, I have the television on in the background and I'm listening to the Israelis bombing Hezbollah's assets in Lebanon—sadly causing the loss of innocent lives. I'm hearing that the United States is worried about Iran and its potential nuclear capabilities and is also dealing with North Korea and its July 4th attempt to launch— or, as it said, "test"—their rockets.

The world indeed is an unstable and volatile playground. But, we've seen this movie before.

Always Go Back to the Cardinal Rules

Worldwide issues and conflicts have been and will always be front and center in the news. Also during this writing, I am listening to the beginnings of what we affectionately call in the business "earnings season"—meaning public companies with a June 30 quarter end are beginning to announce that quarter's results. It's a bit tepid and some companies are lowering revenue and earnings expectations for the third quarter or even for the rest of 2006.

Because of high energy costs, some of the restaurant companies and general retailers are seeing a bit of a slowdown, and some hotel and resort operators are a bit nervous that consumers will trim back on their discretionary spending, potentially carving into their delicate profit margins.

We've had the Federal Reserve Board raise interest rates for the seventeenth time in the last two-and-a-half years to stem potential inflation. It has also stemmed the real estate boom and has tempered the stock market. So all in all, the news is a bit bleak.

But am I optimistic? You bet I am! Am I drinking while doing this writing? Not a drop!

I am optimistic because we have been here so many times, and yet our nation and our economy march on. We have seen the stock market reset the valuation bar, taking stock prices down, then put us right back at the starting gate, ready to run again.

The next cycle becomes exciting—stocks go up nicely in value and then we take another pause. It's been this way since 1900 and the stock market has maintained double-digit returns consistently.

Recall my earlier statement: since August of 1982, the Dow Jones Industrial average has 15-folded. In those 24 years, we have experienced many global and national crises.

Go back to some of the stories in this book about Monster.com, Google, Yahoo!, VeriSign and many others. These companies were not publicly traded stocks in 1990—in fact, they did not even exist. But they are now multibillion-dollar market capitalization companies, employing hundreds of thousands of people.

Remember that one critical, cardinal rule of investing is to stick with a strategy and, as long as the fundamentals are intact, stick with the company.

Easier said than done, but go back and take a tip from the cardinal rules chapter. Examine each company in your portfolio monthly or at least quarterly and whether the stock is up or down, ask the simple questions: has the story changed? Has it gotten better or has there been any degradation? Is the growth rate intact? Have analysts' expectations gone up or stayed the same? Is my broker/adviser on the same page with me? Has the stock become fully valued?

Remember to have an initial price target and re-examine all the core questions once the stock is at or near the initial target. The same analysis should be done with stock mutual funds.

Question the experience and track record of the senior portfolio manager responsible for the stock fund. Be patient, as markets have a way of overcoming all the scary news of the world.

The American entrepreneurial spirit is as alive as it's ever been. I love looking at the major venture capital firms' Websites because the future of the IPO market resides with those firms.

I have close friends who are the general partners of a major technology venture capital firm, and of their 14 portfolio investments, they believe that 4 or 5 of those private companies will be ready to go public before 2007 is out. Another 4 or 5 in their portfolio will more than likely be acquired, since they are better off with a larger parent.

Technology is always evolving, and currently, more sophisticated wireless applications are being developed for both handheld and stationary devices. In the not-too-distant future we will be doing more of our daily computing, reading and transacting in a wireless way, so security applications and devices are capturing plenty of venture capital backing.

Keep in mind from the alternative energy chapter that that sector is also capturing venture capital funding. Americans have turned this once winced-at issue into a serious, needs-to-be-dealt-with issue.

Our children and grandchildren will have different types of energy sources and methodologies. Look back just 20 years: did you think you would have a cheap cell phone that can do so much? Or a laptop with the same power that a closet-size computer had 25 or 30 years ago? Did you think you could compress up to 7,500 songs—the equivalent of 600 to 700 CDs—into a little device called an MP3 player or iPod?

The answers to these questions is probably no—or, "Well, I dreamed that maybe one day..."

Think of the alternative energy space in this fashion. What will be available and standard in 2025 or 2030? Start dreaming—but remember to just follow the money!

Spreading Your Investments Around the World

As Baby Boomers, we are comfortable dealing with and transacting in the global marketplace, which I discussed earlier. With its expansion, we have to be prepared to deal with two motivated emerging giants: China and India. They represent nearly 40 percent of the world's population.

The Internet and telecommunications have brought these two nations along the curve much faster than any one expert could have imagined. By the end of 2006, 3 of the world's 10 biggest banks, as measured by market capitalization, will be Chinese.

The Bank of China's initial public offering was earlier in 2006, and it raised $11.2 billion from the IPO proceeds—an unbelievable amount of new capital. China Construction Bank entered the race with the nation's second bank IPO, and the third will be completed by the fourth quarter of 2006.

These three banks were not on the public stock markets in early 2005, yet they have instantly become global financial forces to be reckoned with.

Capital formation in China and India has made tremendous strides in the past 10 years, as these two nations "get" the global marketplace. With properly capitalized and positioned banks, the growth will not be slowed.

Some will argue that the investing community does not fully trust Chinese and Indian accounting practices. This is true. Many Chinese companies will list on the NASDAQ, NYSE or ASE, and will trade as American Depository Receipts (ADRs), and they must comply with generally accepted accounting principles (GAAP). Those that choose to remain on one or more of the Asian exchanges and not list in the U.S. aren't always getting the best valuation for their companies.

Right now, the best way to invest in the Chinese or Indian markets is to own a mutual fund specializing in them. Refer to the website www.investingbabyboomer.com for more detailed analysis and mutual fund recommendations for these two markets, as well as other global markets.

As we play in the global markets, I hope trading stocks internationally will become easier. Right now, individual investors find it very difficult, if not impossible, to buy or sell shares on the London, Frankfurt or Tokyo Exchanges. Each market has its own set of market-making rules (market makers provide the liquidity in a stock, either buy or sell), accounting rules and regulations, and earnings reporting requirements.

Any company listed on any U.S. exchange must publish its

quarterly results and fully audited financials at least once a year. Companies on the London Exchange must report their revenue and earnings numbers every six months and fully audited financials at least once a year.

However, global markets cannot be ignored. If I asked you to identify the number-one performing stock market in 2005, I can pretty much guarantee you would not guess it. But don't feel bad—I was shocked when I researched it myself.

Ready? It's…Egypt! Yes, you read that right. The Egyptian stock market returned 166 percent for 2005, according to the *London Financial Times.* The second-best performer was the Russian stock market, returning a stunning 125 percent, according to the same source.

Well, that's all terrific and impressive, but how in the hell do you play Egypt or Russia? I work with professional portfolio managers all throughout Europe, advising them on their American stock portfolios, and I cannot get any *decent* research on Russian or Egyptian companies—let alone any that I deem reliable and authoritative.

So, how can an individual investor in the United States get research on these emerging markets?

The answer is that you really can't, at least for now. The only prudent way to play the international markets is to own quality mutual funds that have a history of transacting, and understand their nuances. I cannot certify that I clearly comprehend Russian or Egyptian accounting rules and standards; I leave that up to a portfolio manager who either lives in or travels extensively to these countries and understands the dynamics at work.

But the important point for us Baby Boomers to realize is that our United States stock market, which represented 70 percent of the total world market capitalization 20 years ago, is now is under 50 percent, and it's not the only place to play. We must allocate a certain percentage of our investing dollars to other markets around the globe.

The U.S. market has not been the best-performing market in any of the last 10 years. We buy global products every day; now we must think globally in our investing life. In my personal portfolio, I own shares in the Eaton Vance India Fund, the Eaton Vance Asian Small Companies Fund and the J.P. Morgan Japan fund. I leave the investment decisions up to the professionals on those—the ones who own and participate in the markets.

From Sarbox to London

The London Stock Exchange is becoming the "go to" market for young, emerging-growth companies looking for an IPO. The alternative investment market (AIM) division of the London Exchange has become the new NASDAQ market of this decade—and possibly beyond.

Why? Since the United States endured some horrible accounting scandals in the past few years—*e.g.*, Enron, WorldCom and Adelphia—the government has enacted some very stringent reporting requirements for public companies, falling under the Sarbanes-Oxley Act (referred to as "Sarbox"). It is expensive for a company to file its Sarbox reports, but it does lend a greater degree of confidence to the investing community, so in that respect it is a good practice.

If General Electric spends $5 million to assemble and file its Sarbox report, well, for GE, that's a rounding error. However, if I am a young growth company generating revenues of $15 million per year and I am ready for the IPO market, Sarbox will cost me about $1 million to complete and be compliant.

That is a huge investment for a young company. It is a drain of capital that could be spent on research and development, or on hiring and training additional marketing or salespeople. Sarbox is costing newer growth companies a fair bit of their growth!

So, many American companies are opting to file their IPOs on the London Exchange's AIM market. For example, I personally own shares in a New York-based company called Planet Payment Systems, Inc., which is a leader in the dynamic currency conversion business. It allows you to use your American-issued credit card in a foreign country, and with dynamic currency conversion, your bill is given to you in converted dollars right on the spot.

Planet Payment will do about $12 million to $14 million of revenues in 2006, and $25 million-plus in 2007. Excellent growth story.

Because of the onerous requirements of going public in the United States, Planet Payment instead did so with an AIM listing in March 2006. Its shares now trade on the London Stock Exchange—which has strict accounting/auditing requirements, but nothing as difficult as Sarbox.

For me as an individual investor, it is very difficult to sell this company's shares. I have to contact a United Kingdom brokerage firm who sells the shares and then converts the proceeds to dollars from British pounds. The whole process takes time and money to accomplish—not to mention that I cannot carry the shares in my U.S. brokerage account.

The NASDAQ recently made a bid to buy the London Stock Exchange, but it was rejected. The reason was simple: the AIM market is hot and getting hotter. It processed over 500 IPOs in 2005, while the NASDAQ handled a bit over 200. AIM is taking significant market share and future daily-trading share as well.

As investors, we need to have a strong sense of confidence

in the accounting numbers presented to analysts and investors. The fraud perpetrated by a few in the late 1990s and early 2000s has been dealt with and, in principle, Sarbanes-Oxley is a very welcomed process, but while it's a mere nuisance to a Fortune 1000 company, it is punishing to smaller companies. In short, it's costing us some young growth companies who may be the future of the American markets.

There needs to be a change, and it is hoped that some large, U.S.-based investment banking firms will petition members of Congress to set up two types of Sarbox: one for large, established companies and another that is less expensive and less punitive for smaller growth companies. If we do not modify Sarbox, the consequences will be losing our younger growth companies to the London Exchange's AIM.

Baby Boomers have embraced the global marketplace in their daily lives. But investing in it is still inefficient, so as I said before, the best way to own other nations' stocks is through mutual funds.

Quite often, as the U.S. market is down or trading sideways, other markets are up and gaining momentum, so it's important to have some of your assets placed in foreign-stock mutual funds. The general European markets have typically been undervalued *vis-à-vis* U.S. valuation standards.

There are also hundreds of good emerging technology companies in Asia that are not followed (or barely followed) by traditional research. These companies will have cheap valuations, *i.e.*, low PE multiples in relation to their growth rates.

My Website will have several multinational mutual fund suggestions for you, details about the principal fund manager and, of course, the track record for the past three to five years. Just as my kids tell me, "Dad, think outside the box!" Well, I say, think outside our borders!

A New Definition of "Security"

Social Security is a big, emotional, greatly misunderstood and greatly politicized subject. I will not get into the Democratic party's view or the Republican party's view, because that is a frustrating experience. Any politician knows that Social Security is the sacred cow; any proposal for change sends shivers down voters' spines.

But let's address the issue as simply as we can. The system needs to change—it needs to be revamped. I could write 50 pages of actuarial expectations coupled with life-expectancy assumptions and then throw in rate of return assumptions and blah, blah, blah. But I don't want to lose you as a reader!

Just remember that about 11 years ago, the system was projected to go belly-up in 2017. Congress made some modifications—not to the current recipients' plans, as that would have been political suicide—but to the future recipients' plans, stretching out the retirement age for full benefits from 65 years of age to 67 and raising the ceiling on the payroll tax.

Bingo, we had it resolved. Now the system is due to go bankrupt in 2042, but you know there will be more modifications and a little smoke and mirrors, and it will be fixed. But the remedy will not be permanent.

That whole scenario is a bit scary and Congress can only "temporarily" fix it so many times. The answer is to begin partial privatization of the system. Let people put a portion of their money into a choice of two or three fund types and watch it grow.

Social Security has had a historical internal rate of return of about 2 percent per year—which is terrible and unacceptable. The conservative growth stock funds have averaged about 10 to 11 percent per year for decades.

Think back to when you first entered the full-time work force. Let's say you started at age 23—that's allowing for the one year you spent trying to "find" yourself.

Since then, you eldest Boomers have worked for 37 years and you youngsters have been on the job for 19. If in all that time, a portion of our Social Security had gone into a private account, imagine what would it be worth today!

The money for Social Security comes out of our paychecks automatically; we have no choice or say in this matter. It is the law. Think of the compounding returns these accounts would have accumulated by now. Think of the compounding returns for a new worker who had entered the workforce at the ripe age of 22 or 25. That worker would have amassed a wonderful nest egg and an asset that could have been passed on to his or her children and generations to come.

Revamping the system is not for us Boomers. Our future benefits are in good shape. This is for our children and their children. We should put the fire to the feet of every member of Congress and demand to know how they plan to change the system.

I have spoken with a few actuaries about this issue and found that they were more passionate and emphatic about this than I could ever be. I just wish I had better understood their explanations!

I will get off my soapbox. But, this is an issue that everyone wants to leave to the next generation to solve—or to the next members of Congress. Well, let's demand dialogue from our congressmen and congresswomen, and hope that will bring about some change.

The stakes are enormous for future generations. Most people under age 35 do not believe the system will survive, much less be solvent to pay them their benefits. As Boomers, let's be proactive with this issue as we were in the 1960s and 70s on many other social issues. But first, get a haircut!

Thank you for your time and attention to this book. I hope it has been helpful and fruitful for your future. I invite you to join me at my Website, www.investingbabyboomer.com, which I promise you will be informative and lively.

On my Website, I will explore stock and mutual fund ideas with more in-depth fundamentals, price targets and all the things discussed in this book. I also hope you will especially enjoy my timely interviews with world-class portfolio managers.

I will have ongoing dialogue with doctors and talk about the medicines and therapies they feel will enhance our quality of life. The Website will also feature discussions with alternative-energy specialists, venture capitalists and many other fascinating people.

So, fellow Baby Boomers, we have achieved many milestones and have witnessed the greatest advancements of any generation—not to mention that we are aging gracefully (at least my kids tell me I am). We hope that with more knowledge about health and the prevention of Boomer afflictions, the quality of our lives will be even more productive and fun.

Let's enjoy this quality of life...we've earned it!